Henry Miller Is Under My Bed

MARY DUNCAN is an emeritus pr
University. As a writer, she has been published in *The San Diego Union-Tribune, The Moscow Times* and elsewhere. She lives principally in Paris but maintains an apartment in La Jolla.

The cover of this book incorporates a photograph of the octogenarian Henry Miller, taken by Bradley Smith. The tailpiece illustration is also from a photograph by Bradley Smith. Both first appeared in Miller's *My Life and Times*.

July 1974 — January 16, 2008

For Brian —

Thirty years is a long time. We've both done well. Let's try for another thirty.

With great affection,
Duncan

Henry Miller is Under My Bed

People and Places on the Way to Paris

Mary Duncan

In memory of
Wilber and Mary Hackett
Dixie, Kim and Troy.

© 2008, Mary Duncan
ISBN 0-936315-27-X

STARHAVEN, 42 Frognal, London NW3 6AG
in U.S., c/o Box 2573, La Jolla, CA 92038
books@starhaven.org.uk
www.starhaven.org.uk

Typeset in Excelsior by John Mallinson
Printed by CPI, 38 Ballard's Lane, London N3 2BJ

CONTENTS

1.	Wanting Out	1
2.	Wanting More	9
3.	Belfast: Going in Cold	17
4.	A Defining Moment	25
5.	Not All Adventures Start in Paris	29
6.	Battles on the Home Front	38
7.	Breakfast at Hef's	45
8.	Setting the Stage for Paris	57
9.	Henry Miller in La Jolla	65
10.	Nicaragua: A Close Call	76
11.	There Always Was Sex in the City	87
12.	Khomeini in Neauphle-le-Château	95
13.	A Soviet Union	100
14.	In Simone de Beauvoir's Apartment	112
15.	Shakespeare and Company, Moscow	121
16.	Pursuing Kafka's Last Love	135
17.	Belfast Revisited	147
18.	Henry Miller is Under My Bed	154
	Epilogue: Chez Moi	161

1. Wanting Out

My mother said that my first word was 'mama'. My second word was 'papa' and my third word was 'out'. I crawled to the screen door, pulled myself up and said 'out'. As I grew to be a toddler, I kicked the bottom of the screen until it finally came loose. In frustration, my father nailed a board across the lower part of the door.

Not to be thwarted, I used a toy or spoon to pry loose the screen. Alas, the board eventually covered the lower three feet of my escape route.

We had a small back yard but for some reason I always wanted out the front door, which led to the street. I don't remember these events, but I do remember a man whistling early in the morning at a nearby bus stop. I listened in fascination as its melodic sound lured me into another world.

I had always known that another world existed. I just didn't know what or where it was. It was simply 'out'.

Memories of early childhood include waiting on the sidewalk for my father, Wilber Hackett, a San Diego Transit bus driver, to come home from work. He would slip me a piece of chocolate and wink at me not to tell mother. I also remember my Grandpa Goodman smoking on his front porch and my Grandma Miller's homemade lemon meringue pie. My younger sister Dixie and I would argue over who got to lick the pan.

When I was very young, we moved from San Diego to 1023 D. Avenue, National City, a small blue-collar town closer to the Mexican border. A modest split-level house with two bedrooms and one bath was our new home. In the backyard was a tiny rental cottage. A white picket fence separated it from us.

Behind the cottage was a vast canyon filled with trees, ravines and a small farm that grew tomatoes, string beans and carrots. Eventually the farm was sold and I learned my first environmental lesson as our favorite climbing tree was cut down for a Montgomery Ward's parking lot. I have never in my life shopped at a Monkey Ward's.

Happy days continued for almost a year. They ended when my father died at age twenty-nine from a rheumatic heart. The last time I saw him was at Paradise Valley Hospital; I was four and a half. He offered me a banana from a bowl of fruit next to his bed. Shyly, shaking my blonde curls, I declined.

I remember my aunts, uncles, mother and grandmothers crying in the kitchen while I played on the dining-room floor with my sister and cousins. Aunt Marian asked someone if she should tell me about my father. Coming into the dining-room, she knelt beside me and said, 'Your daddy has gone to heaven.' When I said 'Oh', she walked back into the kitchen and said, 'She's too young to understand.' But I understood.

My mother never recovered from my father's death. She quickly remarried, to Larry Stafford, a charming man who drank too much, womanized and hit her. In spite of their problems, he was always good to us kids. When I was seven, my sister Susan was born.

Larry was a cook on fishing boats. He was popular and generous with the neighbors. A few days before his boat would come in, they would start collecting newspapers. Excitement would grow as we kids anticipated his return and the bounty that would follow.

When Larry arrived, the neighborhood kids would layer our front yard with the papers; then he would set down a couple of dozen large tuna. Amidst the festive air, we would gut, behead and cut the fish into small pieces. No one objected to the stench as mothers carried home tuna to be canned for future use.

The following day, Larry would take us to fish off the back of whatever boat he'd been working on. These days I remember as some of the happiest of my childhood. The fishing industry was dying, however. Money became scarce, and we ended up on welfare. The lack of money led to more fighting and drinking.

Frequently, kids raised on welfare grow up with a different set of values from middle-class kids raised in comfortable surroundings. We were no exception. When bill collectors, truant officers, school nurses, door to door salesmen, plainclothes policemen, welfare workers and people who drove cars with signs or words on their doors arrived on our street, we would play dumb. Anyone wearing a coat and tie, a nice dress or carrying a briefcase didn't belong in the neighborhood. None were good. All were bad.

From this sprouted my anti-authoritarian streak, street smarts and an ability to do the unexpected, trust my instincts and think differently than most white kids. Years later, such survival skills were beneficial in the littered, violent streets of Belfast, war-torn Nicaragua and even Moscow, where I created a business. They would also be vital to surviving in a university.

My family, like some of the countries I would later visit, was full of contradictions, pain and misery. But there was also love, laughter and a strong desire to help one another.

When you are raised knowing and experiencing the problems of not having enough for food and utility bills, you can either accept your fate or learn from the experience. I turned to babysitting and the Girl Scouts for earning money.

The Girl Scouts?

Yes. I was the Girl Scouts' number one cookie seller in National City. I broke all the sales records. The scout leader would brag about me, and my mother was very proud. Then one day the phone rang.

I heard my mother say, 'Yes, I'll ask her.' I knew I'd been found out. 'Mary Rose' – my middle name was used until I went to college – 'How much are you charging for your cookies?'

I'd added a nickel to each box and pocketed the nickels.

The scout leader said I had a choice: I could return the nickels, or I would be banned from the Scouts. It was an easy choice, since I'd already spent the nickels. Merit badges were fine, but money was better.

Life became an overlapping collage of alcohol and arguments, augmented by escapes to Kimball Park with its public library and tennis courts. I would make my own concoction of peanut butter, jelly, honey, banana and sweet pickle sandwiches and head for the library. At dinnertime, I would return, eat and bury myself in borrowed books.

I was an observer, not a participant, in my family's problems. When they became too much for me, my spirit would jump to the small mantel above the fireplace and watch the chaos below. Since I had no physical place to run to, I would run emotionally.

I kept running for many years.

Because of my stepfather's erratic work patterns, my mother took a job as barmaid at the nearby Tahiti cocktail lounge. Young sailors would sit on stools, talking, smoking, joking and telling stories. After school I would walk to the Tahiti and wait for her to get off work at 4:00 p.m..

One of the sailors would seat me on a stool and Mom would give me a coke. On the wall opposite the bar was a large map of the world, covered with red pins. The sailors would mark their hometowns and places the Navy had sent them. With one of their arms round my waist, I would stand on the table under the map and touch pins that designated Hawaii, the Philippines, Japan, Australia, England and of course Tahiti. These were my first geography lessons. They too fuelled my dream to be 'out'.

When I was in the sixth grade, an encyclopedia salesman rang our doorbell. He dazzled us with his beautiful books, and Mother bought a set, on time, paying a few dollars a month. (Only later did I realize how financially difficult this was for her.) *Encyclopedia Britannica*, like the young sailors, took me to new worlds. It also introduced me to the realm of higher education. A photograph of Princeton with its ivy-covered walls drew me in, until a teacher told me that it was for boys only (now it is co-ed). That was the first time I understood the limitations of being a girl. The second came when I wanted a newspaper route. After school and on Sunday mornings, I helped George Gallagher, a childhood friend, fold and deliver papers. When I realized he was getting paid and I wasn't, I told his manager that I wanted my own route. Clearly, I had proven I could do the work. However, girls weren't allowed to have paper routes. *The San Diego Union* didn't want them going out at night to collect money from customers.

During elementary school years, I learned that some kids could not come to our house because my parents drank too much. At first my feelings were hurt; then I decided it was their problem, not mine. I learned early through such discrimination to judge people by their actions and character, not their backgrounds.

My mother further instilled this into me each time she answered a familiar knock on our back door. Standing there would be two or three Mexican men, or wetbacks as they were called in those days. My sisters and I would peer through the curtain while Mom made them peanut butter and jelly sandwiches. She would also give each a quarter, which is what the local bus cost. We didn't have much, but Mom would always share it, saying, 'Never turn away a hungry person.' The Depression Years had taught her that lesson.

When I asked neighborhood kids if the Mexicans came to their back doors, they said no. Later, when I related this story to a friend, he told me that unbeknownst to us our house was probably part of an underground network for illegal immigrants looking for work. They knew my mother would not turn them away or call the police.

Mother divorced and remarried again in order to support my two younger sisters and me. Again, she attached herself to a man who drank too much and abused her. At age twelve I threatened to come into the bedroom where Ray, my new stepfather, was sleeping and kill him with a butcher knife if he ever hit her again. He responded by putting a lock on the door. If he did hit her again, it wasn't in front of me.

Tennis became a way to vent my anger and stay out of trouble. When I was thirteen, I won a tournament sponsored by the National City Kiwanis Club. The local *Star News* called me 'mighty mite', because I was less than five feet tall. Being fast on my feet and having a strong serve compensated for my stature. I would throw the ball in the air, saying to myself 'This is Ray's head', and swing.

I was sent to Arcadia, California, for a major tennis tournament (I lost in the first round) and returned home with visions. For the first time, I had a glimpse of how I wanted to live my adult life. Most of the players stayed in private homes; my hosts had a beautiful house with a garden and swimming pool. They did not impress me so much as the room next to my bedroom: it was a library. Floor to ceiling shelves overflowed with leatherbound books, art magazines, dictionaries, novels and sheet music. My host, a lawyer, found me at three o'clock in the morning sitting on the carpeted floor reading *Oliver Twist*.

At National City Junior High School, I discovered boys. 'Boy crazy' might be an apt description of my behavior. Unfortunately, most thirteen-year old boys were more interested in sports than in girls. Shamelessly, I followed – today we would say 'stalked' – Danny Ellis, who was in my social studies class. At a school dance, during girls' choice, I asked him to dance with me. He accepted, but before the music stopped he broke my heart. Awkwardly, with his arm round my waist, he said, 'Mary Rose, I can't help it if you like me more than I like you.' I fled home crying to my mother, who assured me that I would have lots of boyfriends in the future. Of course I didn't believe her.

Danny, with his teenage wisdom, taught me a valuable lesson, which I never forgot. It is not anyone's fault when one person likes or loves another person more than the other likes him or her. More important, we should not dislike or disparage a person because our affections are not returned. That's life. You have to move on and keep your dignity.

Sweetwater High School is a blur. I remember being in the pompom corps, slumber parties, football games, going steady and being impatient with how long it took to graduate. College would be my passport to a career and personal library full of books. I had no interest in getting married or having children and was appalled when some of my classmates, from so-called good families, got pregnant. I only wanted out.

After graduation, I worked as a summer clerk for San Diego Gas and Electric and saved one thousand dollars for college. Having been admitted to San Diego State College (now University), I knew that I would never make it through if I lived at home, where arguments and drinking continued through the night. By continuing to work part time, I could afford to live near campus. But before that happened, fate intervened.

My sister, Dixie, who was barely sixteen, told me tearfully that she was pregnant. Dixie, who had never been book-smart, had a vibrant, outgoing personality. Everyone liked her, including her teachers, the truant officer and the vice-principal. Always in trouble for ditching school, smoking or sassing adults, she could make people laugh even while they were scolding her.

Would I tell Mother she was pregnant? Of course.

Mom, who was upset, told Ray, who I knew coveted my thousand dollars. He and my mother convinced me to pay an attorney to get the baby's father to provide child support; they promised to repay me before college started. As the saying goes, 'You can't get blood from a turnip'. The father never paid support, and Ray and my mother didn't reimburse me. Mom was too afraid to confront Ray about it for fear he would leave her, and us, without an income.

I stayed home my first semester and borrowed tuition and

money for books from Grandma Hackett, my father's mother. At the same time I applied for a student loan, which I received for the spring semester.

Good grades in high school had always come easy for me; regretfully, I anticipated the same for college. But between the chaotic home environment and my thriving college social life, my grades for the first semester were 0.82, based on a 4.0 system. That is not even a 'D' average. Thankfully, my loan was based on my high school grades. It took two years of good grades to pull the 0.82 up to over a 'C' average.

During that period, Kim, my beautiful niece, was born. Mom welcomed her into our small home, and eventually she moved with her mother into a small apartment. Dixie, like my mother, quit school – she was in tenth grade – to become a waitress and barmaid. After she died of cirrhosis of the liver in her forties, I discovered that her favorite activity when business was slow at the bar had been to do *The New York Times* crossword puzzle.

We never doubted that our mother loved us. She worked hard, always encouraged us and did her best. An attractive woman without a high school degree and no real skills, she survived by getting married and working at various low-paid jobs. This instilled in me the drive to get an education and never be dependent on a man.

With my student loan, I moved away from home and joined a sorority. At last I was out, living in a sorority house and going to college. And now that I was out, an incredible thing happened. I discovered that I was not satisfied. Getting out led to wanting more. However, other than getting a college degree, I wasn't yet sure what *more* was.

2. Wanting More

As a student at San Diego State, I became guilty of 'been there, done that'. Once I had tried something new, I was ready to move on. So it was probably inevitable that I would not be successful at sorority life.

During the 1960s and '70s when sororities were still in fashion, I pledged to one out of curiosity, even though I was usually not a joiner. Being accepted into a college sorority compensated for not having been accepted into one in high school. High school sororities were kid stuff; this was the real deal.

With my thousand dollar loan, I moved into a sorority house. The differences were startling when compared to home. We had dinner at regular hours; there was a curfew; the table was set with linen and flowers; we had quiet hours for studying; no one yelled; serious complaints were heard by a house committee. The sorority represented my entry into what you might call 'civilized society'.

Civilized societies have rules and regulations, though – things I'm not good at. I'm not sure why, but I love flaunting rules – not in an outrageous, illegal or deceitful way but in a humorous, in-your-face sort of way.

The first rule of the sorority, which seems arcane now, was to be in by midnight. I had never had a specific hour for bed, let alone a curfew; in our laissez-faire household you went to bed when you were tired and ate when you were hungry. A curfew grated on my anti-authoritarian soul.

Our housemother, a tippler, fell to sleep fairly early. There was a sign-in and sign-out log, however; it included whom you were with and where you were going. Even though I always signed in by midnight, the housemother complained about me to the disciplinary committee. She strongly objected to my 'double-dating'.

For me double-dating didn't mean going out with another couple; it meant signing in at 10:00 p.m., then going out again at 10:15 p.m. with another date. Many of these dates were not romantic but simply with good male friends. Our housemother felt it unseemly, but for me it was just maximizing my time so I could study during the week.

I ran into trouble with other rules too. Our pledge class (probationary new members) was obliged to clean the house at the end of the semester and purchase a gift, such as new china, for the sorority. After a successful fund-raiser we had enough money for the gift, plus some left over. I talked the pledge class into a mini-revolt: instead of cleaning the sorority house, we hired a cleaning company and sent it to do our work. In addition, we threw a party at the fancy El Cortez Hotel, swore our sorority sisters' boyfriends to secrecy and invited them. I convinced the other pledges that, if we stuck together, the sorority couldn't afford to throw us out, but I was to learn a lesson about group behavior: you're only as strong as your weakest link. Two pledges buckled under pressure, and I got fingered as the instigator. The sorority did not appreciate my leadership skills, and I was de-pledged.

The sorority became the first of many examples of getting what I wanted, wanting more and then moving on. I was so hungry to experience what I'd read about or seen on television or in movies that I seldom had the commitment to continue on a long-term basis, unless there were something long-term to be gained. Acquiring a college degree was one such goal and more important than a social life.

Somehow – I don't remember the details – I moved into an apartment near campus with two friends, Lois and Janie. They were good roommates and tolerated my messy bedroom. I paid more rent than they did to have a room of my own, a thing you couldn't have had in the sorority house. Virginia Woolf might have approved, if there had been room amidst the mess to think or to write in.

College was a happy time. I was learning, making friends, growing intellectually and making money. In a college literature class I first heard about Henry Miller and a dirty book he'd written called *Tropic of Cancer*. Much to my disappointment, no one seemed to have a copy. I had no idea then what role Miller would play in my existence a decade or two later.

When my loan ran out, I started working as a waitress at Carnations restaurant near campus. Three nights a week I worked the 5:00 to midnight shift; then I'd ride my bike home, sleep and get up for classes. From the job I learned some good, transferable skills, such as remembering customers' names, their favorite foods, budgeting time as well as money and knowing that a smile was worth a bigger tip. It was in Carnations too that I met my future husband, who was five years older than me. He ordered a hamburger and asked me out to a movie. Until him, I hadn't dated customers.

He was driving a turquoise Ford convertible in those days. I hate to admit that a car was the attraction, but it was.

We started dating and fell in love. I made love for the first time in the back seat of that convertible. I didn't know yet that a man couldn't keep doing it indefinitely.

'That's fun.' I said. 'Let's do it again!'

'Well, um, I have to wait a little while.'

He and his Midwest farm people represented what I had never had: a stable, respectable, church-going family. I married him for that as much as for himself. My Catholic relations were not thrilled when, during my senior year of college, we walked down the aisle at the Wesley Methodist Church; I, who had been a lapsed Catholic for years, didn't care. Wanting more was becoming a reality. Somehow I knew deep down in my thirsty mind that this was only the start.

With my husband, who was a chemist, came a rented white house with the proverbial white picket fence. I tasted my first martini, hosted my first dinner party with horribly overcooked food and met the wives of other scientists whose husbands also worked at General Dynamics. Within six months, I was bored stiff. A neighbor told me about a part-time job with the San Diego Park and Recreation Department, so I became the after-school recreation leader at Prescott Elementary School in Old Town, San Diego.

Even though my sports teams lost all their games (except one default), I thrived in this new, open, unstructured, fairly unsupervised environment. It led to a full-time position at Southcrest Park, a black, low-income area. Despite the fact that I was white, the kids and I clicked. When social workers, cops and truant officers came around asking questions, I would become the dumbest recreation leader they'd ever met. Never did I give out information about the kids or their families. Unbeknownst to them, our similar backgrounds had created a bond.

All of this was disrupted when my scientist husband got religion. He decided he preferred working with teenagers in the Methodist Youth Fellowship than with test tubes in a lab. So we both quit our jobs and moved to Berkeley, California, where he entered Pacific School of Religion, a liberal, non-denominational seminary.

During the next four years, I worked in the recreation departments of Oakland, El Cerrito and San Mateo and at the same time earned a masters degree in recreation administration at San Francisco State. These years were like being on a joy ride to another universe. I grew intellectually and gained invaluable experience in providing recreation programs to middle and low-income communities.

After my husband and I both graduated, the San Diego Recreation and Parks Department hired me back as a District Supervisor, responsible for one tenth of the city. I didn't realize then that this was my avenue back to San Diego State. After guest-lecturing in several classes, I was invited to be a part-time lecturer in the Department of Recreation Administration. When I was offered a full-time, tenure-tracked position two years later, I didn't know what tenure was. But I'm a fast study.

Bob Hansen, a senior professor, explained the academic facts of life to me: publish, publish and publish. I could hardly believe I was getting paid for what I loved doing most. After research and writing, teaching appealed to the ham actress in me. Now I had a captive audience. The only dreary part of my fabulous new career was the departmental and university committee work, which most faculty members complained about.

San Diego State was like a family in the early 1970s. Faculty, students and administrators were on a first name basis. If you had a problem, you could wander into an office without an appointment, and everyone seemed to encourage everyone else. As the university grew, so did the problems.

Bruno Geba, a dynamic colleague, had a philosophy which impacted on my attitudes about academic ardors. When the department or university was embroiled in some controversy, he would say, 'It is only a zit on the face of life. In a few days, no one will care or remember.' At the same time, he counselled that if an issue were going to matter six months or more than a year later, we should pay attention to it. Amazingly, most issues never mattered that long.

Anyway, the main thing that mattered to me then was 'the gold ring'. When I was little, my father would hold me in his lap as we rode a pony on the carousel in Balboa Park. A long metal arm held out rings for people to grab onto; whoever got the gold ring received a free ride, so my father would say, 'Always reach for the gold ring'. At San Diego State, the gold ring was becoming a tenured, full professor.

Like most successful ventures in my life, I had a plan. I tithed ten percent (a concept learned in church) to professional travel and research. Along with some financial assistance from my dean, I paid for airline tickets to India, Iran, Kuwait, Bahrain,

England and Northern Ireland, plus some other countries. When invited to speak at Oxford University or the Smithsonian Institute, I would pay my own way.

Being a tenured professor meant you were at the top of the pay scale. Because of seniority, it usually enabled you to teach your preferred courses at your preferred hours. Faculty members who had not paid their dues referred to it as 'entitlement'. I went from being a part-time instructor to a tenured, full professor in eight years.

I had the gold ring.

I was also a minister's wife through most of the 1970s. My husband got a job as a youth minister in a rather affluent neighborhood, and we lived in a large parsonage on a tree-lined road. Having been raised Catholic, I wasn't sure what minister's wives did, so I coped with insecurity by teaching, writing and continuing my education. All were acceptable reasons for not being too active in the church.

The liberal denomination to which we belonged was on the cutting edge of social problems. Issues such as ordaining homosexuals, women's rights, racial injustice and the aftermath of the Vietnam War permeated into my rather placid social attitudes. I had been too busy surviving to be aware of larger issues. Now I was becoming aware.

In an attempt to assimilate into the church community, I became active in the women's movement, which initially I had some trouble relating to. It became interesting to me once I noticed that woman's sexuality was part of the agenda. At a retreat for women, films sent by the Glide Memorial Church of San Francisco were shown. Approximately twenty-five of us ranging in age from seventeen to eighty-two sat in a large cabin watching graphic shots of a man and a woman making love on a blanket in a park, two homosexual men kissing and making love in a bedroom, a man ejaculating and a woman masturbating. I realized that maybe sex was one area of my life that would never bore me.

Where did the church women go on to from there? We went to Berkeley, where in a parlor at the Episcopal Church across the street from the Pacific School of Religion we learned to examine our bodies. I'm not talking about our breasts, arms and legs, but our vaginas, inside and out. The Women's Health Center of Los Angeles, which had recently been raided for showing women how to treat yeast infections with natural yogurt, sent up two volunteers equipped with various gynaecological tools.

One of the volunteers explained how, since our reproductive organs were internal and we couldn't see them, we were dependent on doctors to tell us if anything was wrong. But now she was going to change all that. Her colleague jumped on a large wooden table, laid back, lifted her skirt, whisked off her panties and spread her legs. Shocked, we looked on in curiosity and embarrassment. With the help of a speculum like doctors use in their examinations, a mirror and a flashlight, our teacher showed us how to inspect ourselves. Nor was that the end of it.

After the colleague had slipped her panties back on, she sat on the edge of the table and asked, 'Who's next?'

One by one, every woman examined herself while the rest of us watched. Between the Glide films and the speculums, I knew what Helen Reddy meant when she sang, 'I am woman, hear me roar...' To add to her rhyme, I left Berkeley still wanting more.

One of the minister's wives, Ruth Brown, a literature professor at San Diego State, introduced me to Simone de Beauvoir's *The Second Sex* (1949), a feminist's treatise which gave a comprehensive view of women's development in society. From Beauvoir I discovered the concept of 'alterity' – the problem of living life through a man. I was also introduced at that time to Colette, a very different kind of French writer who explored the feminine and sexual aspects of relationships in her stylish novellas.

During those years long before the internet, I buried myself in these books at my university's library. Reading about these

French women who lived in hotels, had lovers, were independent and wrote, I felt a deep envy and curiosity permeating my subconscious. What was their world all about? – In the meantime, however, my husband and I were both working full-time and living in the parsonage.

Growing restless, I suggested we invest my salary in real estate and live on his. I'd achieved much intellectually and professionally; now it was time to gain financially. Following my grandmother Hackett's advice – when I was seven, she'd told me that if I bought property when I was young, I could have anything I wanted when I was old – over the next few years we bought, renovated and sold four homes in Idyllwild, a small mountain community near Palm Springs. Except for plumbing and electrical stuff, we did all the work ourselves: painting, hammering, knocking out and constructing walls, building decks and stairs. This would provide a financial foundation for us.

I was teaching, renovating houses, helping teenagers at our church and becoming radicalized by my women's group, while working on a doctorate at the same time. San Diego only had two universities that granted doctorates in those days: University of California at San Diego (UCSD) and United States International University (USIU), a private institution that had once been part of Cal Western University. UCSD only took full-time students, which eliminated me; USIU hired prominent retired faculty from prestigious schools such as the University of Chicago, Yale and Brandeis and designed its curriculum for working professionals who wanted a Ph.D.. Classes were taught by Viktor Frankl, author of *Man's Search for Meaning*; Herman Kahn, a futurist; Ashley Montague, an anthropologist; Max Lerner, a writer who would later play a central role in my career, and several others. The students were motivated adults with valuable work experience, and their contributions were frequently as important as the professors'. In this environment I would flourish and embark on a research journey that would change my life.

Wanting more had become dangerous.

3. Belfast: Going in Cold

My heritage is Irish. Being Irish is a mixed blessing. The bloodline was half alcohol with all the problems that flowed from it, but it gave me an enduring fascination for all things Irish, including the Irish Republican Army and Northern Ireland.

During prohibition, my Irish bootlegging grandfather bought off the local police in Cincinnati, Ohio, but wasn't successful with federal agents. One night they raided his large two-story house across the street from the Catholic Church and threw all the bottles out of a second-floor window. The lawn must have twinkled in the moonlight like snow. Grandfather barely escaped out the back door. He kept going until he bumped into the Pacific Ocean at San Diego. Four months later he sent for his family, which included my mother, then ten years old.

Mom remembered sitting around the kitchen table with her brother and sister, practicing writing their new name. Moorehead became Miller, and Miller it remained. To this day, Miller is on the gravestone of my grandmother, and Miller is my mother's maiden name. Henry Miller might have enjoyed this bit of Prohibition-related intrigue. Maybe it partly explains my eventual fascination with him.

My interest in Belfast began innocently enough. Drummond Abernathy, a visiting speaker at San Diego State, was discussing playgrounds and recreation facilities in Britain. In an aside, he mentioned that in Belfast the recreation staff had terrible problems because the playgrounds were in a war zone. Bullets, bombs and blood had become more fun and exciting than soccer or table games.

This simple statement galvanized me to launch a research project that ultimately changed my way of thinking, established friendships still dear to me and helped to destroy my marriage. A few months after Abernathy's comments, SDSU gave me $356 airfare for a research project, and in July 1974 my plane was landing in Belfast amidst bunkers and machine gun-toting soldiers, poised for trouble.

The airport bus drove through stop-and-search areas; armored vehicles patrolled the streets; bombed buildings stood as grim reminders of prevalent violence. I arrived at my destination – Queen's University – armed only with a reservation for a student room, notes on the crisis and the address of the Belfast Adventure Playground Association, a non-profit group. There were no friends or colleagues to greet me.

After settling in, I went to find the Playground Association. It provided me with a map of its six playgrounds, three in the Protestant zone, or the Shankill, and three in the Catholic Falls Road area. The administrators I talked with informed me that they rarely ventured into Catholic areas because they were too dangerous. Years later, when two detectives from the San Diego Police Department asked me about Belfast, I retold this story. Amazed that I hadn't had contacts or a thorough knowledge of the city before my arrival, they looked at each other and said, 'When we go undercover into a criminal area with no informants, no friends for back-up and little understanding of how things function, we call that "going in cold". It is not recommended.' I replied, 'Well if I ever write a memoir, I'll call it "Going in Cold".'

Going in cold in this case required four things: a tape recorder, a camera, a notepad and a lot of naïveté – any of which could get you shot or killed in a war zone. Not knowing better, I walked into Divis Flats, a high-rise, public housing stronghold of the Provisional Irish Republican Army (Provos). It had a playground for children. When I arrived, they were practicing for a community vaudeville show, singing 'California Here I Come'. What an icebreaker! Within minutes they had surrounded me and were asking questions about movie stars, beaches, sunshine and Hollywood.

The kids and their families soon adopted me, and I was having tea in their apartments and hearing stories about 'the troubles', as they called the disturbances. If I stayed late, I'd spend the night sleeping in a double bed between two sisters, aged three and six. The three year old was a bed-wetter. Since water rolls down, I got soaked every time.

One evening after a small bomb had exploded, rattling the windows of the Divis Flats apartment, I commented that those damn bombs never went off while I had my tape recorder on. The next afternoon while sleeping in my room in a Queen's University apartment, I was awakened by another bomb. Grumbling, I got up and joined my housemates in the kitchen. One of the young women looked startled and said, 'A couple of guys came by for you, but we didn't know you were here so they left.' Figuring that it was my young Provo friends, I walked over to Divis Flats. As I came in the door, Sean, obviously disgusted, said to me,

'Where were you at 3:00 p.m.?'

'Sleeping,' I replied.

'Did you hear the bomb go off at 4:00 o'clock?'

'Yes, it woke me up. So what else is new?'

Shrugging his shoulders, he smirked, 'Too bad. T'was for you and your tape recorder.'

This was Irish chivalry. Instead of sending candy or flowers to a woman they liked, these young Provos had literally blown up a deserted army lookout so it could be recorded and included among my research materials.

One night a four-year-old girl was accidentally shot and killed in a crossfire by the Provos as she attempted to run from her small house to her grandmother's across the narrow street by the

Divis apartments. Another funeral – those senseless, senseless funerals!

A few days later when I heard gunfire and saw soldiers down on the street, dodging in and out of doorways, I said, 'Oh No, How long is this going to last? I have an appointment with a Queen's professor.'

The others chuckled and weren't much help, but one named Frankie left the apartment and returned a half hour later to say, 'Mary, when you see a woman with a baby pram walking down below, you have fifteen minutes to get out of Divis. If you get shot, it'll be by the Brits, not us.'

About ten minutes later a woman appeared all alone, pushing her baby buggy. Scampering down the cement stairs, I headed for Queens, aware of soldiers hiding in doorways. The Provos had ordered a temporary cease-fire so I wouldn't be late for my meeting.

Twenty-two British soldiers had been shot or killed from the windows of these Divis apartments before I had arrived in Belfast. When soldiers were in the area, no one stood looking out for fear of being mistaken for a sniper. We stood to the side, staying out of view.

Around the time of the baby-buggy episode, the Europa Hotel, known as the 'most bombed hotel in the world', was bombed again. These bombings, which eventually numbered more than thirty, created extensive property damage but never seriously hurt anyone, due to the evacuation procedures established by hotel staff and security forces.

For the Provos and their supporters, each bombing was an occasion for celebrating and drinking at the Felons Club, so-named because most members had to have served at least one year in Her Majesty's prison for offenses against the government. The 'felons' considered themselves better than 'ODCs', Ordinary Decent Criminals such as bank robbers or pickpockets.

That type of bravado was characteristic of 1974. But those

were early days. The Provos hadn't yet formed into their highly effective cell structure, the classic terrorist model implemented when a group feels itself facing serious infiltration. Once organized, a cell would be composed of four or five people with one specific task. No single cell would know what others were doing; thus, if arrested, cell members couldn't give the police too much information.

My short stature, being a young American woman with a friendly smile, and my obvious inexperience combined with the Irish macho culture helped to keep me from being fingered as a 'tout' or informer, even though my reasons for being in Belfast must have initially appeared too bizarre to be true – an assistant professor from San Diego researching the impact of 'the troubles' on children.

These troubles, as I understood them, had started after traditional skirmishes between IRA and Protestant extremists had suddenly escalated in 1968. Soldiers had been sent from Britain to quell fighting and restore peace, but after two years of bloodshed, on August 9, 1971, the government had imposed internment, a form of martial law. More than 200 Catholic men and teenagers had been rounded up during early morning raids; dozens of predominately innocent detainees had been beaten and imprisoned. Frequently, specific charges weren't filed and access to lawyers not provided. The perception of British over-reaching resulted in the Provos acquiring dozens of new recruits*.

Normally complacent grandmothers would leave their backdoors open for men on the run. Catholic doctors would treat gunshot wounds on kitchen tables. Electricians would become bomb-makers; children would run messages; mothers would carry guns and explosives in perambulators, under the blankets of their babies. Taxi drivers were the eyes and ears of the Provos when they weren't transporting arms or wounded men. Nearly everyone became involved.

---

*Much later, the British government would more or less acknowledge its errors by paying financial settlements to some of these men.

On the evening of August 8, 1974, Richard Nixon announced he was resigning from office. It was around 2:00 a.m. Belfast time. In Divis Flats, we watched the soon-to-be ex-President on telly while hundreds of Divis residents stood below protesting internment, holding hands around a large bonfire and singing 'We Shall Overcome'.

By then, I had acquired a lot of chutzpah. Asking indiscreet questions had become a kind of specialty. It often provoked direct, honest answers.

On that night in the Divis apartment I asked an incriminating question of a visiting neighbor, Mack*, who knew me through his young children, whom I'd met on the playground. 'What's it like to kill someone?' I put to him.

Questions like this are best asked after midnight, sitting around a table where rapport has been established, several beers have been consumed and defenses are down.

Mack gazed up from his tea and said, 'You look at the uniform, not the man. You pull the trigger. You don't stop to think he has a wife and children like you do, or you couldn't do it.'

That was when I learned that nice people could be killers.

What drives a person to take lives for his country or cause? In Mack's case, it had started on August 9, 1971, when internment had been imposed. But not everyone among the Catholics I knew in Belfast turned to violence. Many felt that the ballot box was preferable to bullets and bombs. Even before internment, the Irish Republican Army had split into factions over the issue. As early as 1969 those who advocated violence had formed the Provos while the other side had become the Official IRA. Blood had spilled between these two groups at the same time as the Provos mounted their bombing offensive against British forces, which also killed innocent civilians.

After two months in Belfast, I returned to San Diego, an anx-

---

*Names of individuals have been changed.

ious husband and my teaching. Not long after, a letter arrived for me from Belfast telling me that one of my friends had been sentenced to two years in Long Kesh, the British prison nearby, for harassing British soldiers and other crimes. Whether he was guilty or not, I started to send him monthly packages of cigarettes, chocolates and *Playboy* magazine.

When I next returned to Belfast in '76, not much had changed. The Divis flats still teemed with Provo members; Sinn Fein, the political wing of the IRA, had improved its offices and, even though they were no longer in a cigarette-littered room with a clattering teletype machine, the staff was still pretty gruff to uninvited visitors. British soldiers still patrolled the streets; women still banged trash can lids on the pavement to warn of the soldiers' presence; the Europa Hotel, symbol of the British establishment, was still being bombed regularly and, after each bombing, Provos would still celebrate with a few pints at the Felons Club. Life for me, however, was a little less expensive that summer. When I handed the taxi driver money for the ride, he said, 'This one's on me. Be off with you now.'

Once this had happened several times, I mentioned it to a friend, who told me, 'You remember those cigarettes, candy bars and *Playboy* magazines you sent to Long Kesh? Well, most of those drivers have spent time in Long Kesh and some shared those packages. Word's out that the wee Yank [a reference to my stature] gets free rides this summer.'

At Divis flats, a jovial atmosphere greeted my next arrival. Cookies and tea were consumed as five of us caught up on the latest personal and local news. Then after about an hour, one of the women, a grandmother, said to her three year old granddaughter, 'Show Mary what we do to British soldiers.'

The blonde, curly-haired child, who had been sitting on the carpet eating a biscuit and playing with a rag doll, set her things down. Standing, she looked at me and pointed her trigger finger at the window. 'Bang Bang. Brit Brit. Dead Dead.'

Everyone except me laughed and applauded.

'Good girl, Megan. Good girl.'

It was as if her grandmother had asked her to recite a short nursery rhyme or sing a little song for their guest.

Before my eyes, the transference of sectarian hatred passed from one generation to another. The child's mother had been a young teen when I'd first come to Belfast; her father had been in prison for terrorist activities and her mother, this granny, had been on the run. Neighbors had cared for her. Now she was a mother herself and *her* mother, home at last, was teaching her daughter to hate and kill British soldiers.

Where would it end? No doubt their great-grandmothers had done the same thing. In Northern Ireland, this was one of the phenomena that would lead to many more years of violence.

The next time I went to Belfast would coincide with the death of Joe McDonnell, fifth of a group of hunger strikers to die because they refused to wear prison clothes and wanted the right to associate with other prisoners, govern themselves and participate in education classes taught by themselves. The British government was adamant in its refusal to give in to their demands, countering that they were criminals and terrorists, not prisoners of war. The Provos won the propaganda war, but ten men eventually starved themselves to death for their cause.

4. A Defining Moment

After those early trips to Belfast, most problems I faced seemed like opportunities for growth rather than possibilities for failure. I savored the adrenalin rush whenever I was confronted or challenged. Now the gold rings instead of being attached to an iron bar on a child's carousel were dangling from the ends of imaginary red balloons in the air, tempting me to grab onto them whenever they oscillated into reach.

The next gold ring was not an event or a place but a person who further broadened the life of the woman emerging from the streets of National City. My research and writing had led to invitations to academic conferences. The Danforth Foundation invited me to join their Associates Program, established to improve teaching and learning in universities. More than a hundred professors met in Palm Springs for a weekend filled with workshops. The opening ceremony would feature a prominent keynote speaker.

Following introductory cocktails, we all adjourned to a room with round tables set for eight people each. Slightly insecure, I sat at an empty place and hoped someone nice would come join me. Eventually, an elderly man with wild, gray, curly hair strolled up and asked if anyone was sitting at my table. When I nodded no, he sat down beside me, asked my name, what university I came from and what I taught. I explained my course dealing with the social and cultural aspects of leisure and work; he asked what books I used. I mentioned Thorstein Veblin's *Theory of the Leisure Class*, Max Weber's concept of the 'protestant work ethic' and Aristotle, who had much to say about leisure. Not only was he familiar with these materials, he replied, he had written and lectured about them. After a half an hour of give-and-take, I asked his name. It was Max Lerner, the syndicated columnist and keynote speaker.

We talked all through dinner, until a waiter asked if we would like to adjourn to the next room where the others had begun dancing. Startled, we looked around and found we were now entirely alone. Neither of us could remember even introducing ourselves to the other people at our table.

Taking my arm, Max led me to the dance floor. We had danced three dances when he whispered, 'I see you are wearing a wedding ring. Is that a problem?' Knowing the implication, I blushed and said yes. Not long after I bolted, but by then it was too late. We had already created a small scandal among the other academics.

Intimidated, I avoided Max for the next two days. But after the conference he started calling me at the university and we would talk for an hour or so at a time. His secretary started sending me his columns with little personal notes attached. Then Max started inviting me to join him at other conferences where he was speaking.

When it came to men, I had led a rather sheltered life. So when Max invited me to join him at Esalen, a humanistic retreat in Big Sur with a pretty scandalous reputation for nudity and marijuana, I was flustered. He described comfortable cabins in the woods overlooking the Pacific, hot tubs, wine and time to get to know one another.

'Max, I'm married. I can't do that!'

'I'm asking you, not your husband, god damn it.'

I didn't go and, after a couple of months, Max stopped calling me. His secretary, however, continued sending the columns. Eventually, a year or so later, I saw a small article in a paper saying that Max Lerner was going to be teaching on Friday evenings at USIU, only some fifteen miles from where I lived. Like a moth to the proverbial flame, I could not stay away.

I sat in the middle of the large lecture hall and at the break approached him. 'Hi Max, remember me? I'm Mary.'

'Of course I remember you!' – He smiled.

'Max, I would like to interview you for an article about work and leisure.'

'Call my secretary and set up an appointment.'

We both knew this was a ploy – a successful one at that, because the article, 'A Conversation with Max Lerner on Work and Leisure', was published a month or two later.

Naturally, Max started to call me again. I kept refusing to meet him for dinner, but finally we arranged to have lunch at the Westgate Hotel, an elegant place in downtown San Diego. No sooner had I sat down than he was asking me about my current research and what books I was reading. Systematically, he set about seducing my mind as a prelude to the body.

Leaning back in a French provincial dining-chair, he mused, 'Mary, what do you think a woman wants from a man?'

I stuttered. I wasn't sure. I was feeling intimidated again.

Taking one of the yellow legal tablets he always carried with him, Max said, 'Let's see if we can figure it out...' He then proceeded to outline ten commandments (the use of a religious term with a minister's wife was not lost on either of us) that he felt a woman wanted in a relationship: 'Claim her... Be tender... Talk, communicate, connect... Be physical: touch, hold, embrace... Express emotion, give yourself... Address her mind... Take her work seriously... Show strength, but don't hog it... Trust her... Finally, Cleave to her.' After he'd finished, Max wrote across the top of the page, 'For Maria, with love always, Max.'

He called me Ma-ri-a after the song 'They Called the Wind Maria' because, he said, I was like a soft wind that blew love into his life. Very corny, but it worked. I still have his handwritten *billet-doux* to this day.

I didn't know at the time that Max, like Veblin, was a notorious womanizer. When his article 'What a Woman Wants from a

27

Man' was published, he confessed to me that two other women thought he had written it for them.

A week later he sent me a note with a selection of essays by Ralph Waldo Emerson and a book of poems by Edna St. Vincent Millay. – Max never forgot that sharing his mind was his greatest asset.

We started meeting in L.A., at a friend's apartment in Westwood. Yes, I was still married and a minister's wife. Max, in his seventies, was more than twice my age, but I didn't care. Freudian psychologists might have something to say about this, in view of the early death of my father. Max, however, was far more than a mere paternal substitute.

When he had been asked after World War II to describe America in one word, Max had replied 'Access' – access to the country's great institutions of learning, access to its growing economy and access to the tools for creating a life for yourself and your family. And that's what Max gave me – access. Access to an intellectual and diverse life.

Max became where I wanted to go, and he was willing to help me get there. In the process, I never had to abandon my own dreams and desires for an adventurous, independent existence. Indeed, shortly after meeting him, in what started as a routine lecture tour, I would find myself in the middle of a seismic, international political event.

5. Not All Adventures Start in Paris

In December of 1978, I was at a conference in India. It was the best gig I had yet planned, one opportunity parlaying itself into others. An invitation to speak at an anthropology conclave in New Delhi had become the leaping-off point for an around-the-world tour, from San Diego to Hong Kong, New Delhi to Tehran, Kuwait to Bahrain and back to New York. It was my version of what Microsoft would later call 'bundling'.

Sleeping in a squatter village, meeting Indira Gandhi, driving around with an Indian television crew photographing the student riots that followed her arrest, I hadn't been following the news of the outer world – this was the era before CNN and widespread use of email, cellphones and blackberries. As a result, when I stepped off a Pan Am flight to Tehran on Christmas Day, I didn't have any idea I'd be walking into the beginning of the Islamic Revolution.

I didn't know that in October, two months prior to my departure, the French government had coordinated the arrival of Ayatollah Khomeini, his family and entourage to move into three small houses in Neauphle-le-Château, a Paris suburb. Khomeini requested modifications to the properties – new phone lines and structural changes to the bathrooms which, according to his beliefs, didn't point in the right direction. (In *The Little Green Book*, specifying how his followers should conduct themselves, he had stated that 'when defecating or urinating, one must squat in such a way as neither to face Mecca nor to turn one's back upon it'.) The town, with its usual French bureaucracy, said it would take months to get proper permits, but the French Foreign Ministry, not normally concerned about toilet etiquette, stepped in to hasten the process and got the local phone company to install two telex machines and six long distance lines. Khomeini soon had direct contact with supporters in Iran and throughout the Islamic world. In a period of months, he gave over 130 interviews, greeted a hundred thousand devotees, raised money and plotted his return.

That Christmas Day when my plane landed in Tehran, the terminal was filled with hundreds of anxious travellers, each seeming on an important mission. Standing with my bags, I looked for but did not see a friendly face from the university bearing a sign reading 'Mary Duncan'. My lecture tour about the Irish Republican Army was to last four days; then I'd fly to Kuwait and Bahrain where I'd be discussing the same topic as well as consulting on 'Creating Recreational and Cultural Activities for Women in an Arab Culture'.

After thirty minutes, I began to feel that something was not quite right. The mood of the place seemed too frenetic. The biggest warning sign was that no one else seemed to be looking for or greeting new arrivals. Then it occurred to me that only one or two other people had departed from my Pan Am flight. Rather strange for a large capital like Tehran.

Standing there alone, beginning to be bewildered, I started to wonder about how to use the public phone. I was searching in my purse for the number of my hosts when an American voice asked, 'Did you just get off of Pan Am?'

He was a middle-aged man, with a mid-western accent, informal clothes, modest potbelly and thinning hair.

'Yes,' I replied, 'I'm waiting for someone to pick me up from Tehran University.'

'Lady,' he said, 'nobody's going to pick you up. We're in the middle of a damned revolution.'

My mouth fell open. 'What do you mean?'

'Khomeini's people are all around us. They hate Americans and we're in a jam. I'm trying to get a flight out of here, but they're all full. Someone probably paid $5000 for your seat.'

I had just gotten off the last Pan Am flight into Iran while thousands were trying to get out. Two days later on December 27, 1978, Pan Am would suspend all flights into the country.

'What are we going to do?' I asked, with emphasis on *we*.

He looked around, spotted a wooden bench and nudged my bags and me towards it.

'Sit here and watch our luggage. I'm going to check out the airlines again. If anyone approaches you, play dumb and for God's sake, don't speak English. Be deferential and lower your eyes. They're used to women acting like that.'

He walked off, then abruptly turned around and handed me two packs of American cigarettes.

'If soldiers harass you, hand them these; but don't smile.'

Ten minutes later, three young soldiers with peach fuzz on their faces were standing in front of me. They looked inexperienced, but their guns were real. Why, I wondered, do I always end up with a gun in my face?

One started to chatter at me in Farsi; I shrugged my shoulders and looked down. He touched my knee with his short rifle. Startled and afraid, I looked up, quickly reached into my pocket and handed them the cigarettes. Then I looked down again.

They walked away.

After dispatching the soldiers, I sat there unhappy with myself for violating one of my cardinal rules: 'Always pack light with only carry-on luggage'. Sitting at my feet was a large new duffle bag filled with silver wine goblets, woven paintings, new clothes – souvenirs for friends and family. The bag would never reach my next destination. Reality was sinking in.

Frightened about what I'd walked into, I fretted more and more about how to get out. Knowing very little of the situation, I awaited the return of my new friend, about whom I also knew nothing, not even his name.

He returned after about forty-five long minutes.

'Well, Honey,' he said, 'there's no way we're going to get out of here today. Welcome to Christmas in Tehran.' Reading my thoughts, he added, 'A hotel is out of the question. We can't afford to miss a flight or an opportunity for one.' He sat on the bench and introduced himself.

His name was Jim. He was a chicken farmer from Nebraska with a large contract with the Shah's government to raise chickens in Iran. He was getting out now because of the violence he had witnessed in rural areas.

My bladder and stomach started to panic.

'Where are the bathrooms?' I stammered.

Jim pointed to the side of the building and reminded me not to speak English.

The large bathroom was clean, with shiny white tiles on the walls and floor. The similarity to a Western facility stopped there. In the middle of the floor was a tiled hole and on the wall a hose. I was wearing slacks and pantyhose. Since I didn't know where Mecca was, I didn't know if I was squatting in the right direction.

When I returned to the bench, Jim smiled and asked, 'How did you do?'

I chuckled nervously. 'Men do have some advantages. But now that I've solved that problem, what about food?'

Tehran must have good food, but it wasn't there at the airport. Having already staked out the place, Jim said there was only a kiosk serving hot tea and hard cookies. Rummaging in his bag, he pulled out four Hershey bars; not to be outdone, I contributed two apples from my bag. With this bounty, combined with hot tea and hard, tasteless cookies, we sat on our bench and ate Christmas dinner.

Periodically, Jim would make forays to the ticket counter to see if he could beg, borrow, steal or even buy two tickets. He kept coming back with a scowl and hunched shoulders. To pass time, I told about my big plan of travel. When I got to the point of saying that my Kuwaiti hosts would be expecting me in four days, he had a brainstorm. Taking my phone number for Kuwait City, he got an airline employee to call it. A different set of soldiers then came to check us out, but in his easy manner Jim chatted to them in Farsi and gave them more cigarettes, so they left.

We took turns sleeping and watching each others' bags. Our coats became pillows; body fat cushioned our bones on the hard benches.

Morning arrived. More hot tea and hard cookies... Jim started trekking back to the airlines. Success! He had two tickets on Kuwait Airlines.

We hustled our bags to the check-in. He handed an employee money and asked them to call forward to Kuwait. An hour later we were on board.

Food! they served food! We gulped down breakfast, coffee and juice. Jim turned to me and observed,

'You know they're already killing people back there. It's going to be one bloody revolution.'

He was right.

On January 16, 1979, Mohammad Reza Shah would leave Tehran. Two weeks later, on February 1, Ayatollah Khomeini would return to his country from Neauphle-le-Château. Tens of thousands would be executed, killed, tortured or jailed. More tens of thousands would go into exile.

As our plane landed, I thanked Jim profusely. He stayed on board, flew off to Dubai and I never heard from him again. Only later did I realize that being a chicken farmer in Nebraska was probably his cover. How many chicken farmers from the midwest speak Farsi? He was most likely CIA and doing his patriotic duty by rescuing me. Far more than I, he had realized how perilous the situation was.

My University of Kuwait hosts, who had been worried, meanwhile were greeting me with big smiles. We fetched my luggage and discovered my large duffel bag was missing – someone in Tehran was enjoying my booty from India.

A driver in a sleek BMW drove Ganeen, a beautiful young

Kuwaiti guide, and I to the Hilton overlooking the city. When I complimented Ganeen on her stylish, expensive clothes, she said her mother took her and her three sisters shopping in Paris twice a year. Ah, Paris, to be in Paris... But why was an obviously wealthy woman acting as my guide and escort?

Once in the hotel, Ganeen ordered food and drinks from room service with an air that said she had done this often. Sitting down, she asked if she could smoke. Lighting her cigarette with a stunningly exquisite gold lighter, she made me think that if I could light up with that I might smoke myself. Then she told me her story:

In order to get out of the family compound, with separate wings for boys, girls, parents, grandparents, servants, relatives and visiting friends, Ganeen had volunteered at the university to be a guide for foreign visitors. Even though her father let the women in the family dress in modern clothes, he was very strict with girls: they could not go out alone. Kuwait University thus was Ganeen's avenue to social freedom.

During the next few days, in between lectures, she would use me as cover to rendezvous with her boyfriend, smoke and sneak alcohol into the room. She and he would hold hands – nothing more. Our roles were reversed: I became her chaperone. When I inquired about the driver's discretion, Ganeen said he provided the liquor and was well-rewarded for his loyalty.

Touring Kuwait City's modern recreation and sports facilities, I was introduced to various staff. Most were not paid. Doctors, lawyers, teachers and other professional people, mainly men, chatted with the children and teenagers. Because it's such a wealthy country, volunteerism in Kuwait has very high status. Service to the community was expected.

That was one of my surprises. Another was that the dean of the university served wine and drinks at his home.

'A man's home is his castle,' he explained. 'What we do behind our own walls is our business; the government rarely interferes.

It's drinking in public that they care about.'

The dean asked me how much it had cost to get out of Iran. Nothing, I replied: I already had a ticket on Kuwaiti Airlines.

'You must be joking! It's costing thousands to get out of there. The planes are overbooked and many flights have been cancelled.'

My God, the chicken farmer from Nebraska had not only saved me but perhaps paid a fortune to do so. And I didn't even have his card or know his last name.

My lectures about the IRA went well, though the students were more interested in what I had observed in Iran. They didn't want a war spilling over into their wealthy, peaceful kingdom; and their instincts were good.

Eleven years later they were invaded by Iraq.

When my four days were up, I flew off to Bahrain. An American consultant who worked there whisked me off to a nicely furnished two-bedroom government guesthouse in a western-style compound and told me that a driver would pick me up the following morning.

When morning came, stumbling into the kitchen wearing pajamas and hoping to find coffee, I screamed. A man was standing there. Quickly he explained in broken English,

'Please Professor Duncan, I am your cook.'

Mohammed, as he was called, would be there every morning, dressed in white, preparing my breakfast, washing and pressing my clothes, stocking the refrigerator, putting flowers on the table. And when I would return every evening, he would be gone. – Arab hospitality suited me.

My lectures in Bahrain were of a different sort. Sheik Isa, whom I'd met with his wife at a conference in Puerto Rico two years before, had invited me to consult with his government about establishing more recreation, cultural and sports activities for women and girls. What a great job! I was wined, dined, flattered and treated like a princess. An interpreter stood beside me translating my words, which stressed the importance of using the leisure time of wives, mothers and daughters as a way of enhancing family life.

After ten days of this, just prior to leaving Bahrain, I was sitting in the Sheik's office drinking tea. He thanked me and said that his staff had enjoyed my sense of humor and suggestions for expanding their recreation services. Then he asked if he could do anything else for me.

'Yes,' I smiled. 'Send Mohammed home with me.'

Bahraini hospitality included flying first class. The crowded airport lounge was filled with loud, boisterous American men and two other women behaving with unusual boorishness for international passengers. As we boarded Pan Am, the stewardess – they hadn't become 'flight attendants' yet – greeted me by name. I was surprised, until I realized I was the only woman flying first class.

As soon as we took off, the rowdy men started ordering drinks, my seat companion ordering two. The stewardesses ran up and down the aisles with trays, laughing and joking with passengers. It was like a fancy fraternity party. I didn't understand. And why were there only three women on the entire plane?

I soon found out. The other passengers were American oil and construction workers who'd just been flown out of Iran. This was the first onward passage to New York City. A fourteen-hour flight, it eventually ran out of alcohol. No one slept; everyone was hyper; people were trading stories of fear, survival and the joy of going home. Many back in Iran had already died. These men felt lucky to be alive.

When the captain announced that we were approaching JFK USA, with an emphasis on the latter, the plane erupted into cheering and clapping. I was exhausted, and tears flowed from my eyes too as wheels hit the tarmac. A lone voice in the economy section had started singing 'God Bless America', and we all joined in. 'God Bless America, land that I love./Stand beside her and guide her...'

Over two hundred grateful passengers filed off onto American soil. Meanwhile, the Ayatollah, still safe in Neauphle-le-Château, was leading prayers and phoning Tehran. Not long after, he would be flown on a chartered Air France jet to be received by hundreds of thousands of his cheering countrymen. In a classic instance of 'the law of unintended consequences', Western hospitality towards one man resulted in changing the face of the Middle East radically.

6. Battles on the Home Front

Despite this first-hand introduction to the big political issue of the day, my mind was on pressing domestic problems. Back home, I was about to undergo my own personal revolution. I was leaving my husband.

Like political revolutions, personal revolutions require planning. Prior to departing for India, Iran and the Gulf, I had rented a two-bedroom apartment near the university. After quietly and emotionally explaining to my husband that I was leaving, I had moved my clothes, a couple of paintings and my books. I purchased some basic furniture and started my new life as a single woman. I had also recently become the chair of a university department in trouble.

There's a saying that there are wartime generals and there are peacetime generals. I'm a wartime general who gets bored when things are too quiet. I don't go looking for trouble, but if it comes to me I'll stand up and fight. Street smarts kick in. Fair play gets left on the playing field when your role models are the Provisional IRA and Saul Alinsky, the celebrated community organizer.

In the late '70s, as a result of the oil shocks and ex-Governor Reagan's crusade against pinkos in higher education, California was experiencing budgetary problems, especially in the universities. At San Diego State our relatively new president had set about cutting and merging academic departments, including mine. Recreation administration was viewed by the ignorant as equivalent to basket-weaving or finger-painting, so it was an easy target. Big mistake. The president underestimated the community and political clout of our small faculty and alumni who had often gone on to work for city, state, federal park and recreation agencies. Many were now in high positions.

The department faculty often did *pro bono* consulting work related to undeveloped land, urban parks and rec services and could call in markers for debts owed. We kept the phone lines busy and generated an irate constituency that rattled the president. Still, he didn't back down.

I called my newspaper friends who had written about my Belfast research and gave an extensive interview about the proposed cuts. My dean sent his associate to tell me to cease feeding these new stories or our department would be merged with a larger department. Two days later I was quoted about it in *The Los Angeles Times*.

The gloves were off. I was tenured and decided to see what this status was worth. I pulled one of my favorite books off the shelf, Alinsky's *Rules for Radicals* (1971).

Alinsky had been in the news in the 1960s and early '70s for his efforts in organizing workers and communities in fights against city halls or large corporate employers. *The New York Times* once wrote that he was 'hated and feared in high places from coast to coast'. When a city housing authority wouldn't eradicate roaches in a public housing project, he had paid children a penny for every live roach they could capture in a glass jar. He and the children had then gone to the authority with jars full, roaches crawling up the sides to the lid with its small air holes. Alinsky declared that if the roaches were not exterminated, he and the children would return to turn them loose in the authority's meeting-rooms.

Roaches were duly exterminated.

After a large Chicago department store failed to hire and promote minorities, Alinsky told the management that during the busy Christmas season his people would shop, ask for the home delivery which the store prided itself on, then refuse the merchandise on the doorstep. Profits would drop as the store's delivery system bottlenecked.

Hiring and promotion policies duly changed.

The city of Oakland, California was so incensed when Alinsky announced that he was coming to organize their ghetto neighborhoods that the mayor declared they would not allow him to cross the city line. Dozens of police officers waited for Alinsky, the press and a few supporters as they traversed the San Francisco-Oakland Bay Bridge. Alinsky presented his birth certificate and passport.

The police and officials backed down.

Alinsky's thirteen rules for radicals included two that particularly caught my imagination: first, power is not only what you have but what the target thinks you have; second, whenever possible go outside the expertise of the target and look for ways to increase its insecurity, anxiety and uncertainty.

Psychologists say that during a crisis we often revert to childhood tactics. Although I looked harmless with my sweet smile, short height and innocent blue eyes, I would take no prisoners when the Irish dander was raised. Our university president, though upset by the bad publicity we were generating for him, was nonetheless proceeding with his plans. Then I got lucky.

While attending the California Park and Recreation Society's annual conference and having a beer with Russell Cahill, Director of the State Park and Recreation Department, I unloaded about our problems.

'What can I do to help,' he asked.

'Are you serious?' – Russ was the number one person in our field, answering only to Jerry Brown, Reagan's successor as Governor, who, with the legislature, controlled the purse strings of the state universities.

I asked him to write a letter of support.

'Done,' he said. 'Anything else?'

Bob Hansen, a senior member of our faculty, had been trying for years to acquire land for a camp for disabled kids. Nothing had worked out, but he had his eye on a state-owned, bay-front property in Coronado, a small city near San Diego. With its developed sidewalks, rest rooms and unused storage spaces, the property's value then was probably thirty million dollars. Cahill's department controlled this under-utilized park.

'Russ, How about flying down to San Diego and waving thirty million dollars worth of waterfront property in front of the noses of my dean and president.'

'How about on Thursday,' he said – i.e., in four days.

I left the conference and flew home to tell our faculty about his impending visit. A letter of support written on Governor's stationery arrived on our president's desk three days later. Incensed, the president called a meeting with our faculty. Then the other shoe fell. Russ Cahill called asking for a meeting with our dean, the president and myself to discuss transferring a portion of Silver Strand State Park to San Diego State for ten dollars a year – an offer the university could not refuse.

After Russ, the dean and the president had toured the beautiful waterfront site, Russ settled down in the dean's office and said, 'Of course this arrangement is only possible if Mary's department starts and administers a camp for disabled people. We have confidence in her and her faculty.'

The dean, who had only been following the president's orders, smiled. He knew this was also an offer the university could not refuse.

As I was driving Russ to the airport later, he asked, 'How did I do?'

'Wonderful! Academy award.'

'Well, I think that averts your crisis for a while.'

'Russ, when can your staff draw up the lease papers?'

Startled, he looked at me and said, 'You mean you really want that land?'

'Of course, and we'll create a camp that we will all be proud of.'

Camp Able was thus born and still operates today.

Alinsky's rules had succeeded: the president had changed course because he had underestimated public support and, as a new president, was on shaky ground when it came to dealing with the Governor's office and appointed officials.

Our department made other gains from the episode too. Even though the faculty was small, it was now represented on all significant university committees, such as promotions and tenure review, academic planning and the faculty senate. It taught us lessons. Most faculty members, unlike the Irish Republican Army, are reluctant to knife someone who is sitting at the same table. But as Henry Kissinger said, 'Among academics in-fighting is so high because the stakes are so low.' We were all prepared now to be more ruthless.

Max Lerner as always was supportive and amused when he heard about my university antics. When I told him of their origin in ideas of Saul Alinsky's, he laughed, saying that he'd had a long friendship with Saul and his wife – indeed, after his wife died, Alinsky had often visited the Lerner's New York apartment to chain-smoke and cry over his loss. The chain-smoking alas contributed to his death in 1972, long before Max could have provided me access to this one of my heroes. But I continued to cherish his rules in my battles.

Organizations such as universities often create their own problems. For several years San Diego State had a severe parking shortage even for faculty members. Parking permits came to be referred to as 'hunting licenses'. The administrators alone had special parking areas and weren't bothered by these mundane difficulties. Each semester I would request a special one-day permit for a guest speaker; each had a stamped signature and blank space for the date. A shop would then photocopy a hundred copies for me, and every day I would simply fill in the date and place the permit on my dashboard. This was done for three years, until new parking structures were finally built.

Since people generally believe what they read, I also started creating my own university forms. Particularly invidious were the forms for curriculum or new class proposals. The curriculum administrator would send a sheet with little boxes checked off asking for more information; each checked box usually meant two or more hours of work. In protest, I created my own form with its own little boxes, asking why this information was necessary. When I was called in and asked where this form had come from, I said it had been in my files when I'd become department chair. The amount of paperwork rapidly declined. Eventually however, as is inevitable with bureaucracies, the university initiated more and more faculty committees, which generated even more forms for other weary faculty members.

Being chair of the department gave me the opportunity to raise its profile both on and off campus. By reassigning a portion of our budget allocated for a faculty position, I was able to establish a lecture fund and start a series of special events and weekend courses for which students could earn one unit of general credit. As a result, whenever I read a book that seemed on the cutting edge, I would invite the author to campus. Philip Slater on *The Pursuit of Loneliness*, Leo Buscaglia on *Living, Loving and Learning,* Marilyn Ferguson on *The Aquarian Conspiracy*, William H. Whyte on *The Organization Man* and of course Max Lerner on *America As A Civilization* all came to speak in this way. Others would follow, until these lectures became the beginning of a West Coast version of Parisian literary salons.

As my six year term as chair came to an end, I created the Institute for Leisure Behavior, an umbrella organization to house all our department's creative activities, such as external publication, lecturing and seminars. For me it would be a platform to continue contributing to the department; however, behind my back another faculty member lobbied the colleagues to appoint him as director of the new institute instead of me, which they did. I did the legwork, he took the prize – a huge, unintended favor. I vowed from that point on to never create something that a vote of the faculty could take away.

Despite such conflicts, I was keenly aware that San Diego State provided me a platform for personal growth and exploration. I may have struggled with its internal politics, but I never took for granted the opportunities that being a professor in a progressive institution could offer. It gave me the latitude to expand my energies and take in friends and places from a wider world, with values and experiences far different from my own.

My journey into that wider world would impel me next into the flesh-pots of Beverly Hills.

7. Breakfast at Hef's

Everyone has a secret garden. For over twelve years, from 1978 to 1991, mine was at the Playboy Mansion West in Los Angeles, California. This was my parallel universe – a favorite place to write, read, study, think and socialize. Only my nearest and dearest knew I was spending time there. Feminist friends were appalled, but curious. My husband, to whom I was still married during my first visits, didn't know. How do you tell your husband, who is a protestant minister in a major denomination, that you are spending time at Hugh Hefner's luxurious estate? You don't.

I had been rendezvousing for some time with Max Lerner in Westwood when he invited me to have lunch 'at a friend's house' near Beverly Hills. 'He has a large art collection, antiques, a pool and a tennis court,' Max said. 'Bring an overnight bag in case you would like to stay.'

I drove up to a large iron entry where a male voice came out of a gray rock asking me if he could help. I gave my name and the gates swung open. On the way up a gently curving road, signs warned to be careful of children, animals and Playmates. Once at a circular drive, a butler opened my door. He told me I could find Max Lerner by the pool.

With his curly hair and pug nose, Max was easy to spot, sitting on a terrace writing his column for the *L.A. Times* syndicate. After greeting me, he told another butler we were ready for a late lunch and ordered two small steaks with salad. I still didn't know where I was, but I was certainly curious. As we were eating, a man approached wearing pajamas. Max waved and called out, 'Hef, come and meet my friend Mary.' Though his mother called him Hugh, Hefner was 'Hef' to his pals. Graciously, he welcomed me to Playboy Mansion West. Then he walked off.

'I teach Hef about sex,' Max quipped, 'and he teaches me about politics.'

The two had met in the 1960s when both were on a television show to discuss changing sexual standards in America. Hef had invited Max to the Mansion in Chicago, in whose luxurious surroundings the famous and infamous met, mixed and sometimes mated. Art Buchwald was also invited that weekend; his wife wasn't pleased, but he was curious about what went on and couldn't stay away. Max recalled Art entering a pool in a cloud of steam, not being able to see and hoping that when the cloud dissipated some raving beauty would be coming towards him. Alas, it was only Max Lerner.

For the six years during which I was the chair of my department at San Diego State, I visited Max at the Mansion. My able male secretary, Tony Salvador, was the only person at work who knew I wasn't really attending some seminar or other. Max and I would giggle when Tony would call to relay messages from my dean or a faculty member. Then one day the dean insisted Tony give him my number. The Mansion's butler answered:

'Playboy Mansion West. May I help you?'

The dean at first thought it was a joke. Fortunately, he was a bachelor and could be silenced with gifts of *Playboy* magazine, with signed centerfolds bearing personal inscriptions to him.

Max appreciated brains as well as beauty. To the Mansion he imported his own female retinue: two professors, a psychologist and a writer. Max's wife, who lived in New York, was not much more amused than Buchwald's with his visits to Hefner's world, but she accepted that they contributed to Max's well-being as he fought off the cancer which eventually killed him.

Bordering Bel Air and near the UCLA campus, the Mansion had over five acres of gardens, a pool, a lagoon, an aviary, a zoo, a guest house with three bedrooms for visiting Playmates, the

Game Room with three bedrooms for indulging in sexual fantasies and of course the twenty-two room mansion itself with its seven bedrooms, wine cellar, gym, spacious kitchen, Grand Hall, Mediterranean Room, dining-room, den, large living-room that also served as a movie theatre and offices for the magazine staff. The best-kept secret was that intellectual life thrived between the parties, sex romps and movies that went on. While sitting around breakfast table, tennis court or pool, you could often gain first-hand information about books, politics, the film industry and lives of celebrities.

One day as we were sitting and writing near the tennis court, we heard a voice call, 'Max Lerner. How nice to see you here.' It belonged to Bradley Smith, who'd written two books with Henry Miller, including *My Life and Times*, published by Playboy Press. Bradley and his French wife, Elisabeth, were at the Mansion to approve photos for the Playboy edition of his new book, *Erotic Art of the Twentieth Century Masters*.

Max and Bradley had been friends in New York twenty years ago. They caught up on old times and people they knew. The list was impressive: Tennessee Williams, Truman Capote, William Faulkner and Margaret Bourke-White, as well as Miller.

After the Smiths left, Max told me about Henry:

'He was the greatest erotic writer and affected me very much. *Tropic of Cancer*, *Tropic of Capricorn,* a whole set of autobiographical writings about his life in Paris and New York... I used to smuggle books of his out of Paris and slip them past customs. It was always a problem. Fortunately, I usually met inspectors who'd read my column and they'd let me through. That's how I built my library.

'There was a lawsuit over the books being pornographic and Miller's lawyers asked me to come to Brooklyn and testify. Three of us testified: the critics Lionel Trilling, Alfred Tate and myself. I had three hours in front of the jury. It turned out the foreman was a reader of mine. Henry got off and wrote me a letter of thanks for saving him from jail. What a silly business.

This was one of the great writers of our times – far better than D. H. Lawrence. You read *Lady Chatterley's Lover* now and it's quaint; Miller stays modern, fresh. What makes him literature is the delineation of the people. His people emerge. Every one of them is alive. And that's what great literature is.'

Max and Hugh Hefner considered Miller an icon where issues of obscenity and pornography were involved. After Miller won a 1973 Supreme Court case against the State of California, films, books and DVDs began to be judged by the 'Miller test' – i.e., evaluating content based on community standards, sexual explicitness and literary merit. *Tropic of Cancer* had been ruled literature. Prior to that, there had been several other cases against his books, including the 1964 Gerstein vs Grove Press, which Miller's publisher had won. This was the trial Max had testified at.

As we continued to sit by the tennis court, Max explained the concept of pornography to me:

'The difference between pornography and erotic literature is that erotic literature is about human beings. Pornography is mechanical, and that's why you get bored with it. It's repetitive and becomes dehumanized. When I look at a PB centerfold, I think: there is beauty. But if I'm going to read something about sexual acts and it's repetitive and human beings don't emerge, then it is pornography.'

Like most of life at the Mansion, breakfast at Hef's would be casual. At around 7:30 a.m., I would go downstairs dressed in slacks and a sweater and enter the Mediterranean Room next to the kitchen, overlooking the pool and gardens. A peacock might be strutting around or an emu, which occasionally bit people. This limited to some extent going topless in the garden – several Playmates protested, and one day the emu was no longer there.

In the center of a large glass table surrounded by dark bamboo chairs was a small wooden box with a button on top. This electronic device summoned one of the butlers, available twenty-four hours a day. (If you wanted steak and eggs delivered to your room at 4:00 a.m., you used the phone next to your bed and dialled 12.) Prior to more people arriving, I would read *The L.A. Times* or work on an article for an academic journal. But the suspense would be building – who would be first to join me?

Around 9:00 a.m. a couple of Playmates from the guest house might show up for coffee while awaiting a limousine to take them to the studio for a photo shoot. Devoid of make-up, they would be truly beautiful, in the 'girl next door' manner Hef favored. They'd sit for a while and chat about upcoming parties, their boyfriends – rarely allowed at the Mansion – an acting lesson or the latest techniques for breast implants. Sometimes they'd tease me because I'd tell them to get an education and not rely on men for support. Few of them, after all, were on an equal footing with the men who came there. Many were obsessed with the material aspects of life and too young and beautiful to realize how quickly their chances would fade.

After they left, the next contingent arrived. Over the following few hours James Caan, Tony Curtis, Bob Culp, Bill Cosby, Dick Van Patten or Cornel Wilde might appear; occasionally Jack Nicholson or Warren Beatty. Some would be staying at the Mansion, others only coming for tennis, a swim or lunch with a friend. Most were on the 'gate list', which meant they had twenty-four hour access. Sometimes one of them might be using the Mansion as a refuge while he was drying out from alcohol or drug abuse, laying low during a difficult divorce or meeting a lover in a discreet environment.

As in childhood, I became an observer of the realm around me, though instead of in a small house in National City it was a multi-million dollar palace. But if the view was different, many of the same issues prevailed. The rich and beautiful are more like the poor than you imagine. They too wrestle with 'substances', unwanted pregnancies, poor health, lack of purpose, lack of love or self-respect. The main difference is that these guys had resources and alternatives by which to solve their problems.

My favorites at the Mansion were not the stars so much as the writers and directors – Richard Brooks, for example, director of *Cat on a Hot Tin Roof, Blackboard Jungle, In Cold Blood* among others. With his silver hair cut short and wearing sweater, slacks and sandals, he'd usually start his mornings sitting in a side chair reading the paper. But eventually he'd gravitate over to the glass table.

My first conversation with him began with a question about how he'd conducted research for *Looking for Mr Goodbar* (1977), a cult film about a young lonely teacher who goes to bars looking for sex and eventually drugs.

'Actually,' he said, 'it was based on the case of a Catholic woman who taught at a school for the deaf and was brutally murdered. But I couldn't use her because it would have caused too much pain for her family.'

'What script are you working on now?' I asked, seeing that he had put his paper down.

'*Fever Pitch*. It's about gambling. When I was researching it, I almost became addicted myself.

'Did you know that gambling affects over 100 million individuals in America? About 78% are social gamblers: they can take it or leave it. About three percent are professional; they work in casinos and elsewhere. A small percent are criminal gamblers. Then there's the compulsive gambler, eleven or twelve million of them – maybe ten percent.

'Compulsive gamblers are the best liars in the world,' he went on. 'You can tell what's happening with an alcoholic or drug addict but with a gambler you don't know.'

Richard's personal life was complicated, I would discover. He'd been married three times, including to the actress Jean Simmons. According to Max, Richard had also had an affair with Elizabeth Taylor, whom Max knew, having met her in London in 1959. Taylor would tell him years later that Brooks had been his only rival; this was before she'd met the other Richard, Burton.

Max and Richard had had affairs with her simultaneously, it

emerged. But Max had always kept a secret from Liz Taylor, too. One night as he and I were driving to see *Star '80*, a film about the murdered Playmate, Dorothy Stratton, he opened up to me about it:

'I used to go see Elizabeth at the Beverly Hills Hotel – she kept a bungalow there. I'd check into a room and then ring her. I couldn't stay at her place because Eddie [Fisher, her then husband] was around, but we'd wait until he went out to practice his songs and have a late breakfast. Then we'd have lunch. Sometimes dinner. It was very nice. When she left, I'd go on to see someone else – that was my secret... I was visiting Marilyn Monroe at the same time.'

'Max, you're kidding. Where would you meet *her*?'

'Very close by, at her home. It was within a half hour from here; she had a small house of her own. There was no security that I know of – you didn't seem to need it in those days. It wasn't a violent time.'

'So you were seeing both of these colossal stars back-to-back?!'

'I wasn't sleeping with either much, but we carried on a lot. I was fucking another marvellous woman then too. She came to hate me because each time she'd ask when we could meet again, I'd say that I had to see either Elizabeth or Marilyn. Finally, she couldn't take it anymore and moved out of town. Of course I should have held onto her, but I was star-struck. I was a stupid young man.'

Max once escorted Liz Taylor to Paris for a weekend. They spent it mostly at the Deux Magots watching people watch them. This and much more is told in the book *Elizabeth: the Last Star* by Kitty Kelly, who devotes several pages to Max. Max would complain that, when Kelly interviewed him, she had a secret tape-recorder going.

'She kept getting up every twenty minutes or so to go to the bathroom... She made half a million dollars more for that book because of my interview, and all she gave me was a case of wine.

I'd have appreciated a check instead.'

Max felt that Kelly had misrepresented his relationship with Taylor. 'I didn't do anything with Elizabeth that I didn't do with Kitty,' he claimed.

There was, of course, an issue with Max's frequent use of the terms 'affair' and 'goings on'. In another of our many conversations, he contended that he'd had his first affair was when he was four. Sometimes he only meant petting or kissing, not sex. So did he or didn't he have *sex* with Liz Taylor? If you want to know, ask Kitty Kelly.

Writer and illustrator Shel Silverstein, who wrote the children's classic *The Giving Tree* (1969), would visit the Mansion when he was in L.A.. Over breakfast one day he would comment to me that the inspiration for his book had come in a flash and that he'd written and illustrated the whole thing over a twenty-eight hour period.

I often wondered whether Shel shaved his head, like Bradley Smith, or if he were naturally bald. Perhaps, like Bradley, it was a little of both. To offset the baldness, he sported a handsome dark beard and moustache.

Shel told me that he worked on something creative everyday, even if he was only thinking about projects:

'Sometimes nothing comes, but when it starts flowing you have to grab it and go with it.'

Max would join us, and he and Shel would tell humorous stories. One was about Al Capp, the cartoonist who'd created *Li'l Abner*. Shel would ask, 'You remember how Al used to unscrew his wooden leg and shake it at women, trying to get their sympathy so they'd go to bed with him?'

Later Max would explain how Capp, who had lost a leg in a childhood accident, was notorious for his womanizing.

Occasionally, as I listened to some of these yarns, I felt as if I were living between the pages of tabloid magazines. And sometimes, when I was in a grocery store back in San Diego, I'd scan the headlines of them with amused interest, because I was now meeting and conversing with the figures on their covers.

One morning, for instance, Jessica Hahn appeared for breakfast. Jessica was responsible for the downfall of Jim Bakker, the evangelist, in a sex scandal; now she was living at the Mansion to write a book about it and pose nude for *Playboy*. Clearly Hef thought Jessica was important – she was billeted in room number two, the large guest room just down the hall from his own suite.

Jessica was friendly but seemed a bit shy with strangers. She contended that Hef had saved her life and had given her a new start. 'When I arrived I only had a few dollars,' she told me. 'He and his staff have created a home for me. I idolize him.'

I confided in her that I had been a minister's wife – she almost didn't believe me – and talked a little about the positive aspects of church life.

'In some ways I miss all that,' she mused, 'the music, the fellowship, the friends... Now the Mansion is my church, and Hef is my god. He took me out of a hotel and brought me into his home. He protects me from all the bloodsuckers out there; he's given me a new life, and that's what God does.'

As if reading my mind, she eventually added, 'Everyone here is a gentleman – far more than Jim Bakker ever was.'

Hef had another reason for taking Jessica in: he didn't want other magazines scooping her story. She would benefit, though. She went on to earn over a million dollars posing for *Playboy* and later got a part in *Married With Kids*, among other acting and radio work.

Security at the Mansion was exemplary. Dressed in tailored shirts and slacks or suits, the guys would deal with everything from Playmates trying to sneak in boyfriends in the trunks of their cars to putting people who had drunk too much in a taxi or keeping hard drugs off the property. They prevented the theft of art objects and nabbed the occasional intruder trying to climb over the fence; they also protected female guests and Playmates from unwanted male attention. The one problem they couldn't solve was squirrels jumping on the fence around 10:30 every morning. Even though they knew what was setting off the sensors, they always had to run and check it out.

Placed on tables around the Mansion were pencils, note pads and matchbooks with the *Playboy* logo on them. Anyone could take these as souvenirs – my dean received a supply of them. Whether the plush bathrobes in the grotto dressing-room were meant as gifts too, many of them disappeared also.

Upstairs in the Mansion there was a hallway leading to the magazine offices. Along this, between photos of parties and events at the Mansion, were six bedrooms with bathrooms for guests. While little sound was audible between these rooms, moans from amorous couplings often flowed through the doors that led to the hallway. Hef himself held court in a round, mechanized bed that could accommodate up to twelve people. Rarely did he sleep alone. A male guest once wondered what it could be like to be in a room full of beautiful women and know that you'd been to bed with all of them. A Playmate would confide in me that she was surprised Hef had never asked the girls to sign confidentiality agreements.

The Game Room, which was really a house, had the latest in pinball machines, pool tables and refrigerators full of drinks, as well as three 'fucking rooms': the Red Room with a double bed and garish mirrors on the ceiling; the Blue Room with an oval bed; and the Orgy Room with a large round, beige mattress recessed into the floor, with mirrors all around it. Each of these rooms had a bathroom and a lock on the door. Guests could use them at any time.

Once when I was showing a female colleague from SDSU around the Mansion, I took her to the dressing-room next to the grotto and pool. In its center were two very popular items: an artistic version of a gynecologist's examining-table, with leg stirrups designed in chrome and black leather, and a sun-tanning bed. As we walked in, talking about the Mansion and not paying attention to who was in there, we bumped into Harry Reems, the biggest male porn star of the day. He was lying nude on the bed, wearing small eye goggles and a plastic cup over his penis. Hearing our voices, he took off the goggles, turned on a side and said, 'Oh, hi Mary.'

Not knowing any special etiquette for the occasion, I calmly introduced him to my guest. Then we departed.

Bright red and embarrassed, my colleague whispered, 'Mary! how could you do that? introduce me to a naked man?'

'Discreet nudity is a way of life at the Mansion,' I said. 'I've gotten used to it. If you want to see him in film, instead of in person, go see *Deep Throat.*'

After dealing with an alcohol problem, Harry found Christianity and went to sell real estate in Park City, Utah.

Wet t-shirt and wet jockey short contests were popular attractions at holiday events at the Mansion. One male contestant, however, was disqualified when a Chiquita banana label was visible through his white underwear.

Movie nights were buffs' heaven. After dinner for fifty to seventy people and a screening of a Hef-selected film, we would have dessert back in the dining-room. Hef always invited people who'd worked on the film, so sometimes you would find yourself sitting at a small table with the director, producer, screenwriter, set designer or lead actor. All would answer your questions and, if you wanted, conduct an informal seminar about how the film was made.

With the birth of Hef's children Marston in 1990 and Cooper in '91, life at the Mansion changed. A baby-stroller sat in the Grand Hall, a swing hung from a tree, room number two became the nursery and Hef bought a house across the street for the Playmates. When he and the boys' mother separated in 1998, he bought the mansion next door for her and them and installed a gate between the two properties so as to have easy access. As of this writing, Marston and Cooper are teenagers, and Hef lives with three Playmates in what might be construed as a group marriage. The movie nights continue, as do holiday events and Playmate of the Year parties. There is still a gate list – as Max often said, 'Staying at the Mansion is like living at a five star hotel, except you never receive a bill.' For Hef, though, it was not a hotel.

He once said that the Mansion was like a family, but it was also in some ways a modern version of a middle-eastern harem – polygamous without the religious mandates. The women came willingly with their own agendas – to become rich and famous as models, singers or movie stars, say, or to meet a rich husband. Some succeeded; others descended into alcohol and drugs. As a family, Hef's was of the patriarchal kind. He made the rules and controlled the finances. Whoever was his current girlfriend – or later wife – would be mistress of the place, and the butlers, other residents and visitors would cater to her. Other women acquiesced in this: she had her power through association with Hef. But these other women, often referring to themselves as 'sisters', would hang out together, exchange secrets, gossip and commiserate on their condition.

I, who owned a home and had my own means of support, could enjoy the best aspects of the Mansion and feel like a privileged guest, not someone trying to establish a career based on my looks. Still, I wasn't kidding myself. If it hadn't been for Max Lerner, I would never have been there either.

8. Setting the Stage for Paris

Real life went on. By 1980, I had become a full professor and made another of my periodic trips to Belfast. One of my sources there gave me a detailed diagram of the Provos' internal organizational chart, with a complete description of their cell groups. Using that information, I wrote an article for *The San Diego Union*, which was published on October 4th 1981.

A month later my office phone rang, and a think tank in Washington D.C. invited me to participate in a symposium on terrorism, all-expenses paid. I accepted.

As usual, there were more men than women in the room, totalling about twenty people. Everyone was introduced; we all had some specific expertise about which we said a few words. During a break, I was asked for specific information relating to my Provo sources; I answered in generalities. On the second day, a male colleague told me that my questioner had been from the Agency.

'Mary,' he said. 'You're being recruited for the CIA.'

How naïve could I be? The CIA guy returned later and said, if I accepted their offer, all my research and travel expenses from then on would be paid through grants, with the caveat that the Agency had first priority to my information and that all of my articles had to be approved by them prior to publication, even if they were only children's stories. Politely I declined. If we had been in a conflict like World War II, I might have felt different. We weren't.

After Washington, my next trip east was for pleasure – to Paris.

My beginning in that City of Light was not in a garret, cold *chambre de bonne* or bare, bleak hotel room such as described by Miller, Hemingway or George Orwell. My first address there was in one of the most fashionable buildings in the 6th arrondissement, heart of the Left Bank. Andy Warhol lived upstairs part of the year; the owner of Club Med entertained in the penthouse; and during my first week *in situ*, limousines lined the street as elegant guests swept through the large, dark blue wooden double-doors for a party being hosted by the Italian Countess who occupied the west wing of the building.

Dan Dixon was the owner of this place I was so lucky to stay in. Like the city himself, Dan was a mixture of personalities, charm, style, sophistication and generosity to friends. His gestures to me would include giving me keys to all four of his European residences.

My life in the late '70s and early '80s was like a layered cake, each layer filled by new friends with a different perspective on life, each more delicious than the last. After I had left my husband and moved into my own apartment near San Diego State, I had also bought a tiny one-bedroom beach house less than two hours south of the Mexican border. My *casita* provided me with a respite from the university and hectic life I'd created for myself. It was there that I'd met Dan, at a Christmas party.

Dan was a resident of Point Loma, an affluent district of San Diego bordering ocean and bay. He had inherited money and parlayed it into more money through purchases of property in desirable areas of the world. When bored with Paris, he would travel south to Cap d'Antibes on the Riviera where he had a small flat overlooking the sea. Eastward, in Venice, he had a spacious apartment on a canal. From Venice, he might hop over to the four-bedroom place he owned in Sitges, a seaside community near Barcelona. Dan also owned properties in San Diego and Mexico. The decorating budgets of these places seldom included kitchens or bathrooms. In Venice, while the large living-room had marble floors, a pail of water was needed to flush the toilet. But no matter their condition, Dan's homes were always in excellent locations.

Tall, thin, wealthy, eccentric and of a certain age, this magical patron of mine preferred younger men. Frequently, he would travel with young Mexicans from Tijuana or Ensenada who could help restore his various European apartments; in return, they could live in Europe for months of the year. This procedure often caused Dan arguments and diatribes against the U.S. Immigration Department; he had to write frequent letters justifying his need for Mexican workers in Europe or line up at various consulates to try to expedite their visas.

I used to laugh when I told people how politically Dan was to the left of Karl Marx. Notwithstanding his beautiful homes and his money, he seldom had anything positive to say about the 'capitalistic, war-mongering U.S. Government'. He would never acknowledge any paradox between his leftist beliefs and inherited wealth and ability to increase his fortune by real estate investment. I don't know if Dan ever had a nine-to-five job, but I do know that he bragged about two things: first that throughout the Vietnam War period he'd never paid taxes to Uncle Sam, because he managed to borrow or leverage his property so that all the interest he paid to banks could be offset again what he owed on income (never mind that the banks paid taxes and therefore indirectly Dan supported the war); second that he had managed to subvert the army when he was drafted.

While in boot camp, Dan had deliberately peed the bed every night. The sergeants would try to humiliate him in front of his peers, assigning him latrine duty, or punish the entire barracks for his misdeeds; but he'd still wet the bed. They'd withhold liquids from him after dinner, but he'd counter by developing an even stronger bladder so as to hold his urine all day. When the army doctors, sensing a phoney in their midst, challenged his medical history, which showed no record of bed-wetting, Dan claimed that shame had kept him from seeking help previously and that his mother and family housekeeper had always changed his sheets to protect him. Of course this was a lie. But it worked. The army couldn't have a private who peed the bed and disrupted discipline. So Dan had been honorably discharged.

I was never quite sure what was true and what false in these Dan Dixon fables, but I do know he would've enjoyed me repeating them.

Dan's Paris flat was in the Rue du Cherche Midi, a building constructed in 1686, during the reign of Louis XIV, the Sun King, who had built Versailles. Its ground floor had once contained stables for carriages and horses; the courtyard still housed an old Egyptian statue in the middle. It was here, gazing at a pagan god across from what had originally been a stable, that I fell in love with the city.

Giving me his key, Dan refused any money, asking me only to tip the concierge. He also gave me an introduction to an American artist friend living nearby who could help me in my new adventure. On the day of each of my successive arrivals, I had a specific routine: first I would open Dan's long, golden silk drapes to let light into the dark living-room; then I would go out and buy large, pale, pink tulips on the Rue de Buci and put them in an old white vase; finally I would slightly rearrange the furniture to make the place seem like my own. The day would not be complete without one further act: I'd run across the street to Poilane, the bakery, and buy a *tarte aux pommes* – my favorite. In winter when I made this excursion, I would wear a long coat over my pajamas.

Raucous arguments between the concierge and his wife occasionally broke the quiet of my evenings. Otherwise, I would luxuriate in peaceful solitude in the fifty-meter (500 square foot) space. The décor was pure Dan: two nude male cherubs standing two and a half feet tall and looking very angelic despite their erect penises; deep forest-green velvet spreads covering twin beds on opposite sides of the room and serving as sofas; faded but once beautiful drapes framing French doors leading onto a charming interior garden. Leather-bound copies of Miller and

Gertrude Stein lined bookshelves; faded moss-green carpets covered the floor. There was a corner fireplace with mandatory large, gilded mirror over a marble mantel and to one side a large, dark oil portrait of a somber man, which Dan had probably acquired at a flea market. The ceilings were a majestic twelve feet high. They curved.

In a small room between the living-room and kitchen was a double bed, also covered in dark velvet. The kitchen was special. It shared a small interior patio with Andy Warhol's studio and apartment. Dan complained bitterly when Warhol put French doors onto this patio without consulting him. He also decried how insensitive Warhol's fashion-model guests were, walking on the marble floors above him in high heels.

On two occasions, Warhol and I nodded to each other in the courtyard. Once, after he'd decamped to New York, I bribed the concierge to show me his apartment. Its living-room was dominated by a round sofa, large enough to seat six people; piles of his magazine *Interview* were stacked on the coffee-table. The small bedroom upstairs had a closet filled with colorful, old French jackets and pants looking like they were from the Napoleonic era. Unfortunately, none of Warhol's paintings were on the walls. Maybe he wasn't as narcissistic as the world imagines.

Of other neighbors, only the Italian countess made herself known to me. Her two little dogs would visit when my doors were open and showed their disdain for the American tourist by lifting a leg to pee on the drapes.

In spite of my having the run of Dan's European apartments, Paris was my favorite. With its architecture, café life, literary history, winding sidewalks, wines, food and even smell of strong cigarettes, it drew me. With each trip, my desire to live there increased. I fantasized about redecorating Dan's apartment or even owning it. I gazed up at those tall, curved ceilings or out through the doors into the courtyard, filled with plants and small trees, and it seemed like an impossible dream. Desire was so strong that I completely ignored the lack of sun or natural light in what was really a dark cavern. Looking back, it is clear that I would not have been happy there. The walls were permeated with conflict and sadness. Cherche Midi, I'm sure, was an unhappy place.

I don't know if it was Dan's aura, his psyche or that of some previous inhabitant, but I used to wonder what had taken place there or who else had inhabited the place. Dan once told me that Violet Trefusis, the English aristocrat who had an affair with Vita Sackville-West, thinly disguised by Virginia Woolf in *Orlando,* had lived there in the '20s. I was never able to confirm this. Nor have I been able to verify that another of the flat's prior occupants lost his head in the French Revolution.

Though I appreciated use of Dan's apartment, I began to develop a secret dread that whoever stayed in it would never be happy. Eventually he or she would be infected by a gloom emanating from the walls. In fact, this negative ambiance drove me fanatically to read the real estate section of *The International Herald Tribune* and French newspapers whenever I was in Paris. Each visit I would go and see other apartments, and each one would feed my dream. Most of my first French words were real estate terms.

On one occasion, while trying to locate a flat for rent on Boulevard Raspail, I knocked on the wrong door and Edmond Kiraz, the French cartoonist, answered. Inviting me in, he told me how to find the address I was looking for. Meanwhile, in his living-room, with its panoramic views of the Left Bank, I saw a pile of *Playboy*s on the floor next to an easel. After he'd told me he drew watercolors for the magazine, I asked him if he wanted to meet Hugh Hefner and visit The Mansion; in return, he invited me to Brasserie Lipp for lunch, the restaurant Hemingway mentions in *A Moveable Feast*, famous for its snobbery. Picasso and many other famous writers and artists had hung out there, and now I ate my first escargots there as a guest of Kiraz. Later the headwaiter – remembering that I had first arrived with this famous man – would always give me star treatment.

Making friends in Paris was a slow process, but with introductions I developed a group of peers who shared my love of the place. Year by year my reasons for returning expanded until, gradually, I grew close to my goal.

In 1992, when he was sixty-nine, Dan's throat was slashed with a broken beer bottle by two young men in Ensenada, and he bled to death. They said he'd made sexual advances towards them and, though arrested, were never convicted. A lengthy estate battle ensued between Dan's relatives and charities. His prime properties in San Diego, Venice, the Riviera and Sitges were sold, lawyers pocketing most of the proceeds and the liberal charities to which he had bequeathed everything – the American Civil Liberties Union, the Quakers, Amnesty International and the Mary Knoll Fathers and Brothers – receiving almost nothing.

The battle ate up more than $300,000 on legal fees, with a number of law firms angling to get their share. Two long-time friends, Walt Wysoczanski and Aubrey Thornton, to whom Dan had left an interest in his San Diego home, received only a pittance after it was sold. As one of Dan's old pals remarked to me, 'Never leave lawyers in charge of your estate: they'll get it all.'

Once Dan's Paris flat was no longer available to me, I began staying in a large, luxurious, three-bedroom place in the 5th arrondissement, overlooking the Arena Lutetia, one of the few Roman remnants in the city. For several years I would rent it whenever its owner was travelling, to see her children in Ireland or Australia. The apartment became my Paris home until I bought my first apartment in 2001.

In between trips to Paris, however, I had discovered another vibrant world, much closer. Carved into the cliffs and scenic hills north of San Diego was La Jolla, pronounced 'La Hoya', a small town known as 'The Jewel', although in Spanish it actually means 'the hollow', referring to the cove and caves thereabouts. Whenever my car would reach the crest of Ardath Way – now La Jolla Parkway – and begin its descent into this pretty town, with the Pacific spread out around it, my stress levels would go down.

La Jolla became where my intellectual journey to Paris really began and where Henry Miller became a part of my life.

9. Henry Miller in La Jolla

I should have known that anyone I met at the Playboy Mansion did not come from the conservative elements of La Jolla society. Two weeks after meeting Bradley Smith, I was sitting nude in his hot tub while Elisabeth, his wife, poured wine. Though casual nudity was common at Hef's, I didn't expect it in the hills of La Jolla.

I'd discovered this affluent seaside suburb of San Diego after starting to date Ed Robbins, Executive Director of the San Diego Jewish Community Center. We'd met when I hired him to teach part-time on our faculty. We were both single and incorrigible when it came to bending non-fraternization guidelines. He was renting a handsome ocean front condominium with panoramic views over La Jolla Cove. I was charmed by the place.

We'd walk to the local restaurants, have coffee in a cafe and drink wine in the park. He'd teach me – his favorite 'shiksa' (gentile woman) – about all things Jewish. I ate my first bagel, lox with cream cheese, onions and tomatoes, with Ed. Vividly he would describe the Holocaust and how his family had escaped it. His reminiscences about holidays such as Yom Kippur, Hanukkah and Passover vastly increased my scanty awareness of Jewish history and religious practice.

Ed introduced me to D. Z. Aikens, a deli close to my home near San Diego State. In an attempt to show him I was learning about ethnic food, I'd go there during the busy lunch hour and buy various items. Standing at the counter with its vast displays, I asked for four bagels.

The owner's wife asked me what kind I wanted.

'You mean there's more than one kind?'

'Yes,' she said, pointing to a list.

Among the selection were water, egg, onion, garlic, poppy seed and even chocolate-chip bagels.

'Ummm, I'll take two water and two chocolate chip.'

I thought she flinched when I said chocolate chip. Since I already had onions and tomatoes at home, I also asked for some cream cheese and some of that 'pink stuff'.

Putting her hands on her hips, she shouted to her husband, 'Zeke, a Shiksa has another one of our boys.'

The entire restaurant burst out laughing.

When I told this story to Ed, he put his hand to his forehead and said he could never take me to D. Z. Aikens again.

After my second visit to La Jolla, Ed encouraged me to move there. I rented my home to two friends and took a large studio at 939 Coast Boulevard, an ugly high-rise that La Jollans hated – the building is partly responsible for creation of the California Coastal Commission, which now regulates all construction on California's shoreline.

The attraction to La Jolla actually was not Ed. The first time he met me walking on the beach with Max Lerner, he recognized Max and was star-struck and stuttered as he tried to think of what to say. 'Mary,' he told me later, 'I really underestimated you.' – He had to learn something that other men would: Max came first and, if they couldn't deal with it, they could move on.

Most did.

Six months after moving to La Jolla, I saw an ad in the newspaper for a penthouse condo in Ed's eight-unit building. Without hesitation, I signed a year's lease on it. Ed flipped. I was now living two floors above him, which he felt was too close. We both came to agree, however, that at times it was convenient.

Eventually Ed realized that my motive for moving there was about real estate more than him. A female friend moved in with me, and a year later we bought the place. Our new home was the ultimate in 'location, location, location'. For me real estate was becoming more profitable than teaching.

Ed moved on to San Francisco where he married his Jewish sweetheart. Not long after, while playing tennis, he died from a heart attack. We all were devastated.

By that time I had become a regular for dinner at Bradley Smith's. Bradley was a *Time-Life* photographer and author of twenty-three books, including two with Henry Miller – *My Life and Times*, as I've mentioned, and *Insomnia*, Henry's story of his love affair with Hoki Tokuda, his fifth wife. Bradley's other books ranged in subject from Gandhi to President Truman, erotic art, Arabian horses and a series on the history of countries through their art. *Japan: A History of Japan through Art* had sold over eighty thousand copies.

Bradley's hot tub was known throughout La Jolla. Bathing suits were optional, and most people chose not to wear them. Feeling a little peer pressure, I was initiated into this custom.

The tub was on the end of Bradley's swimming pool and surrounded by plants, murals and sculptures. Some of San Diego and La Jolla's most notable residents enjoyed this aspect of his hospitality. When Bradley would call with a dinner invitation to meet friends, preceded by the tub with drinks, they would almost always accept.

On one occasion when Bradley suggested I bring a male friend, I invited a date I knew to be liberal in respect to going nude in small groups. When we arrived, Bradley, Elisabeth and two guests were already in the tub.

'Mary, you know where the bathroom is,' Bradley yelled. 'You can change there and get towels.'

My companion and I took off our clothes, wrapped up in towels and walked out to the tub edge. As decorum required, Bradley and the others averted eyes while we dropped towels and stepped into the water. Pouring us wine, Bradley then introduced us to the unknown couple.

After a few minutes of chat, I noticed something odd and a little alarming. Elisabeth and the other woman had two small strips of fabric covering their shoulders.

'Elisabeth,' I asked, 'are you wearing a bathing suit?'

'Yes,' she replied in her French accent. 'Apparently I forgot to tell you we decided to wear bathing-suits out of respect for the mayor's new protocol officer.'

My date and I were the only ones naked.

Perhaps to make up for this episode, Bradley called me soon after with another invitation. This wasn't just to any dinner; the other guests this time were Francis Crick, Nobel Prize winner for his participation in the discovery of DNA, his wife, Odile, an artist known for her risqué paintings, and our mutual friend, Max Lerner.

Bradley served the shrimp gumbo for which he was famous, but the shrimp wasn't what attracted everyone's attention. On each of our plates was a black and white painting with various parts of the female body depicted in a sensual juxtaposition to one another. 'Graphic' would be an understatement for the details staring up at us.

An enlarged view of two large breasts attached to a headless torso was on one plate. Another showed a woman's face enlarged on her stomach with her lips dissolving into the pubic area. In 1971 Henry Miller had borrowed Piero Fornasetti's erotic version of that face for the cover of *My Life and Times* – 'a gesture,' according to Fornasetti's son, 'that tickled the crusty old man, who viewed it as the highest form of flattery.'

So it went, around the table.

'It's a shame to cover these with food,' Max laughed.

Twenty-five years later I don't remember everything about the evening, but I do remember the main question. 'Could a computer ever write a Shakespearian play?' Both Max and Francis, fascinated by the newest developments in A.I. – artificial intelligence, as called – took opposing views. It was two great minds exchanging ideas, point and counterpoint, while the rest of us were smart enough just to listen. Their passionate dispute was not personal: each held to his opinion without descending into disdain or mockery. Saying 'No', Max maintained that a computer could never duplicate Shakespeare, using arguments calling on his knowledge of great writers and humanist thinkers. Francis, a true believer in A.I., said 'Yes' and, citing great scientific accomplishments, maintained it was only a matter of time.

Afterwards, I remember thinking 'I wish I'd had a tape recorder.' It was a lesson learned. From that evening on, I carried a recorder with me wherever I went with Max. Later I would add a video camera, and many of the memories and conversations included in this book are a result of the electronic gems I was able to get down accordingly.

It was at Bradley's that I first encountered Henry Miller – not in person, because he died in 1980, but on tape.

One day when entering the house, I heard a booming Brooklyn voice talking about Paris.

'Who's that?' I asked.

'Henry Miller,' Bradley answered and invited me into his office to see his Miller books and photos.

Sitting on the floor, I fell under a spell. All I remembered about Miller was that he had written the infamous *Tropic of Cancer* (1934), banned as porn in the States until the 1960s. Now I could hear him tell in his own words how he and his wife, June, had arrived in Paris in 1928 with money she'd raised by selling his writing as hers to a male admirer. (She'd also sold candy to drunks as they reeled out of bars.) They had toured part of Europe, lived at the Grand Hotel de la France on the Rue Bonaparte and returned to New York broke a year later. With more money raised by her, Henry had sailed back to France in 1930. Over the next few years, while writing *Tropic of Cancer*, he met Anaïs Nin with whom had a long affair. Using her husband's money, Anaïs helped to support him, as June had. Henry was a survivor and the women who loved him helped him survive all the way.

Some think of Miller as a womanizing cad; others admire his ability to write even when cold, hungry and almost homeless – 'almost', because he often stayed with generous friends who didn't have much more than he did. Throughout his life, it was clear that, though he liked and used women, it was not just for sex. In his autobiography as well as on Bradley's tapes, he stated: 'For me sex wasn't an everyday thing. Attached to the woman's cunt was always the woman herself. The woman was the most interesting thing.'

I listened to that wonderful voice reminisce about how Alfred Perles, his best friend in Paris, had shared an apartment with him that became the setting for *Quiet Days in Clichy*; how a prostitute, getting drunk, had stopped to pee in the street; how he himself would tiptoe past hotel clerks so he wouldn't have to pay for a room. I listened to him tell about borrowing money from friends, running up bills in restaurants, searching the streets for someone to feed him – indeed, making lists of friends stating the date on which they would prepare dinner for him, in return for his good cheer and colorful tales.

On the day *Tropic of Cancer* was published, Miller moved into 18 Villa Seurat in the 14th arrondissement. The 14th has a long history of housing literary figures and providing sustenance and warmth in its cafés. Samuel Beckett, Sartre, Simone de Beauvoir, Dali and Soutine all had lived there. – The address added to Henry's allure for me.

Some years later when Bradley was in Paris researching the possibility of a new book on Miller, he took me to visit Villa Seurat. The building was modern by comparison to some of its 18th century neighbors. As we stood outside looking up at a small balcony where Henry had stood, Bradley shrugged, 'We might as well knock and see if anyone's home.' An English-speaking man answered the door and, after Bradley had identified himself as co-author of *My Life and Times*, invited us in. Of course the furnishings and décor had changed since Miller's time, but the apartment was still filled with light. It had a very high window and an attractive garden with large green plants. It was easy to see why Henry had enjoyed his four years here. We tried to imagine Anaïs, Alfred Perles and his many other friends drinking, smoking and making love in this corner or that.

On Bradley's tapes Henry lamented how the coming of world war forced him to leave Paris and accept an invitation to visit Lawrence Durrell in Corfu. He wanted to stay in Greece, but visa issues caused him to return to New York. Feeling even closer to him by this juncture, I listened to him chat about how he'd hated his life in Brooklyn, his mother, working with his father in a tailor shop, the kids he had known and an older woman he'd lived with for several years, whose heart he had broken. He left her, he said, without even leaving a note. Then he met her again years later – she was an usher at a movie theatre – and she said to him, 'Harry, why, why did you do it?' In his gravelly imitation of her tone, you could still hear the pain.

Henry married five times, had three children, wrote books dealing with sex, painted, loved Paris and lived in Pacific Palisades, an affluent part of Southern California, for the last twenty years of his life. In a lot of these details Bradley's life paralleled his. Bradley also married five times, plus one annulment. He had four children, wrote three books related to sex and erotica, was a photographer, visited Paris many times and lived in La Jolla, a fashionable part of Southern California. Both men had become bald; both defied societal norms, Bradley having quit school at age twelve, starting a one-page newspaper in Texas and buying a camera. Both had friendships with people in common, including Erica Jong, author *of Fear of Flying*. Bradley's third wife, Helen, had discovered *Fear of Flying* in a La Jolla bookstore where she worked and, knowing Henry through her brother, had Bradley send him a copy. Henry reviewed it for *The New York Times,* comparing it favorably to *Tropic of Cancer,* which caused sales to increase dramatically. When Henry told Bradley that he'd posed fully clothed in bed with Erica Jong, Bradley photographed him doing the same with Elisabeth.

Feminists such as Kate Millet criticized *Tropic of Cancer* as being misogynist and anti-female. Well, maybe. But at least today's authors have the freedom to express themselves more openly and intimately because of it.

On the tapes Henry pointed out that he had overlapped with the 'lost generation' of the '20s, including Hemingway, Fitzgerald, Ezra Pound, Picasso and numerous women writers such as Djuna Barnes and Gertrude Stein. He didn't really socialize with them, he says, preferring Tolstoy, Gorky, Schopenhauer, Mann, Nietzsche, Huxley, Darwin and Spengler. Talking affectionately, he went on to tell about how he moved in the early '40s to Big Sur, where the isolation, surf and forests agreed with him. He mentions Dr Murphy, the owner of Esalen, and how he enjoyed the hot tubs there with Murphy's family and friends. He says he found peace of soul in Big Sur and so stayed for some fifteen years.

How I coveted these tapes of Bradley's! Never did I tire of listening to them. Then came a day when Bradley invited me and a couple of others to Big Sur for the centennial of Henry's birth. There we were surrounded by Miller's family, friends, fans, books and photos. First edition or signed copies of his other works – *Tropic of Capricorn, Big Sur and the Oranges of Hieronymus Bosch, Black Spring, The Time of the Assassins, Wisdom of the Heart* and *The Smile at the Foot of the Ladder* – were all available. The last two, which didn't deal with sex but were more philosophical, were apparently his personal favorites. I bought copies of several.

A consummate storyteller, Bradley always enjoyed an audience, and Henry wasn't the only notable person he had known. His memories of Margaret Bourke-White, the *Life* photographer, have never been published. When her biographers asked him about their relationship, he would discuss only her professional merits. To friends, however, he would reminisce about how they had met in Bombay, in 1946, when each was covering India and Gandhi.

Bradley had hired a porter to carry his bags into his hotel. Unfortunately, while taking a shower, the porter stole all of his clothes. When Bradley called down to the desk for assistance, all they could tell him was that there was a colleague of his also staying at the hotel – perhaps she could help. A phone conversation later, Margaret Bourke-White – Maggie, as he called her – was standing at his door with a set of shirts and a pair of pants over her arm.

The chemistry between them was immediate. They danced most of the night on his terrace overlooking the city. Next day she took him to a tailor – but the relationship didn't end there. They became lovers and remained friends until she died of Parkinson's disease in 1971.

Maggie was proud and tough, Bradley would tell me. When her illness was in full swing, she might fall on the path in her yard yet pick her self up to continue. It was one of these falls that eventually led to her death.

Bradley particularly admired her spunk and ingenuity in coverage of World War II. Maggie would often beat her competition because she managed to get generals to fly her in military aircraft to where the action was. When other editors would complain or criticize reporters for not getting similar or better articles, they would protest, 'Maggie has equipment we don't have.' Asked if she used sex to get her material, Bradley would laugh and say,

'This was long before women's lib. She combined wit, charm and sex appeal with photographic genius to combat the old boys network and ingrained bias against women journalists and photographers. More than one male journalist had slept with a general's secretary or even wife to get an advantage over the competition. They only complained when Maggie did it to better advantage – such as when she flew in the American bombers as they destroyed Germany.'

Bradley's strong voice would soften when he recalled what really bound them together. Both had an affinity for the poor and exploited. He compared Maggie's photos from *You Have Seen Their Faces* – a book she did with her husband, the writer Erskine Caldwell – to his own sequence on Southern sharecroppers.

Bradley's generosity spread to everyone he knew. He would loan books, video- and audiotapes, money, art and his own photographs. Most valuable were his introductions. He truly enjoyed matching friends, not romantically but intellectually. Once he knew your interests, he would always have someone you needed to meet.

In 1982, for example, when he heard I was returning to Paris, he regaled me with more Miller stories and insisted that I meet some of Miller's old Paris friends. At the top of the list was George Whitman, owner of Shakespeare and Company. Bradley wrote a letter of introduction, saying I was an expert on the IRA, a writer and dear personal friend; would George invite me to Sunday tea and, if necessary, provide me with a bed? That letter established a pattern of behavior for me. Ever after, when arriving in Paris, Shakespeare and Company would be a first stop. It is what Henry described as 'a wonderland of books.'

At the Shakespeare and Company across from Notre Dame, I would learn about Sylvia Beach, owner of the original Shakespeare and Co at 12 rue Odéon. Later, I would meet Beach's namesake, Sylvia Beach Whitman, George's daughter, who would eventually run the store. Others I met there include Ted Joans, the beat poet, who invited me to Sunday dinner to meet Jim Haynes, an American expatriate in many ways the doyen of the Left Bank community in the '60s and after. Through these connections I came to realize how inclusive and family-like the expat community in Paris can be to strangers.

Besides Whitman, Bradley provided me with an introduction to Eugene Brun-Munk, a distinguished, colorful Hungarian 'count' who enjoyed good food and other men. Eugene was an editor for Stock, the French publishing house, whose owner, Christian de Bartillat, had published Henry's *Insomnia*. Eugene had also worked with James Jones.

Like Edmond Kiraz, Eugene would invite me to Brasserie Lipp. We'd sit in the back and he identify journalists, writers, film directors and politicians as they came in, including President Mitterrand. On one of these occasions I learned that Mitterrand had a mistress and no one really cared. Eugene said, 'Oh, there's Mitterrand. He's with his wife tonight, not his mistress.' – Only two security men stood at the door.

According to Bradley, Eugene had a secret you'd never guess from visiting and drinking champagne at his luxurious apartment, with its red linen walls, in the 7th. He'd been born poor in a small town in Texas. Only after working his way through college had he changed his name, recreated himself and moved to Paris as a *mittel*-European count. Nor was it until I read Bradley's files that I learned of his connection to Miller.

Ah, the missed opportunities!

Every newcomer to Paris needs a social anchor. Bradley also introduced me to a couple living on Avenue Foch in the affluent 16th who welcomed me into their home and for twenty years listened patiently to my dreams of moving to Paris. Before that, however, I had other things to do and places to see...

10. Nicaragua: A Close Call

In 1985, Dan Dixon made me an offer I couldn't refuse. He needed a property manager for Villa Surf, his ocean front estate in Point Loma. When friends told me I was crazy to leave my La Jolla apartment, I invited them to visit my new home.

Surrounded by a hundred acres of city park land, Villa Surf had three cottages and a house with an eight hundred square foot living-room. After moving in, I installed a hot tub on the brick terrace. For five years, the acre and a half site was the scene of parties and literary events. Bradley Smith agreed that I had the only hot tub in San Diego that could compete with his.

From Villa Surf I ventured down to Nicaragua, which like Belfast had become a war zone. The Somoza family, installed by the United States in 1936, had ruled the country with ruthless methods and amassed a fortune until 1979, when the Sandinistas – originally peasants and students – overthrew them and their allies. Because of the new régime's leftist ideology, the U.S. cut off aid to the country and commenced supporting the Contras, an anti-communist guerrilla organization.

During the '80s both the Sandinistas, now supported by the Soviet Union and Cuba, and the Contras, supported by the U.S. and various right-wing groups, were heavily armed. Each accused the other of atrocities against civilians. Each was correct. Most of the violence was in rural and border areas, not major cities. The middle of the decade was complicated by the Iran-Contra Affair, in which the Reagan administration was discovered selling arms to Iran and using the proceeds to finance the Contras, both of which had been made illegal by the U.S. Congress. Iran, ruled by Khomeini, needed funds for its war against Iraq; meanwhile, somewhere in the black and white arguments made by the Contras and Sandinistas was a wide swath of gray.

The gray is what stoked my curiosity. It was also partly a consequence of my Belfast research. How were the children being affected? Did they go to school? What role did the teachers play? Could the children go out and play safely in their neighborhoods? Were the government and other groups politicizing them? What was actually happening in the rural areas? – The press didn't address these questions adequately, let alone answer them, so I wanted to go see for myself. As usual, I was going in cold.

Most of the passengers on my flight to Managua in the summer of '87 were either journalists or members of non-profit aid groups. The passport control officials collected your thirty dollars, stamped your visa and in my case typed in the words 'Managua', the capital, and 'Leon', the second largest city. These were the only places I was legally allowed to visit.

I didn't know anyone and had no contacts. The only hotel ever mentioned in the press – the Intercontinental, where journalists, businessmen and visiting government officials stayed – was too expensive. Back in San Diego the 'Friends of Nicaragua', a group that sent volunteers to build schools and work on other humanitarian projects there, had recommended a hotel for seven dollars a night. It turned out to be clean, centrally located and with a private bath, but lacking in air-conditioning. Its low cost meant that I could fund the trip without outside finance.

Applying for grants was anathema to me by now. Grants meant paperwork, frustration and probably 'no' for an answer. After my first Belfast trip, which had been funded by a small stipend from SDSU, I'd started funding my own research. Applying for grants ran the risk that the most important moments of a conflict might pass by while you were waiting for a reply. But research was essential if you wanted to be promoted to full professorship, which meant substantially more income. In the end

I kept the administrative stuff to a minimum, knowing that my research would eventually more than pay for itself.

This strategy paved the way for lots of international travel and participation in conferences. Two of my university deans, Max Howell and Jerry Mandel, were enthusiastic supporters of my projects. My high profile invitations almost always encouraged them to find some travel money for me. Besides, they always received a bottle of their favorite liquor from the duty free shops. Saying thank you is important.

Two props usually worked as introductions for me when arriving in a war-torn country: a current *New York Times* and a *New Yorker* magazine. Within a couple of hours of landing in Nicaragua, I was sitting in the Intercontinental chatting with Jake, a reporter from Boston, and Craig, an aid worker. Sharing my props with them provided me with a current appraisal of the war, the location of the press briefings and parties, a free lunch and new friends to bail me out of trouble to come.

Inquiries regarding the border areas brought a shrug of the shoulders and the disappointing information that it was impossible to get to them without special visas and an airplane. Craig mentioned that he was leaving the next morning to visit one of his projects and that there was an extra seat on his flight; the obstacle was that visas were always checked. If I could have a proper visa by 7:00 a.m., he could take me.

It was now Sunday afternoon.

Challenges are like red flags to a bull for me. Passport control had used an IBM electric typewriter with a revolving ball to type 'Managua' and 'Leon' on my visa. The Intercontinental had the same kind of typewriter in an office behind reception. How to gain access to it?

At that time the average Nicaraguan earned the equivalent of four dollars a month. A pretty female clerk had already answered some questions for me and appeared flexible, a characteristic prevalent in troubled communities. Approaching her nonchalantly, I explained the problem. She hesitated, but looked longingly at the twenty dollars I showed. She asked me to return in two hours when she would be less busy.

Two hours later we were standing over the typewriter with a photocopy of my visa. Slowly we rolled it in. After selecting a font, we typed 'Esteli' next to 'Leon'. Wrong font; clearly a forgery. Partial success came on the second try: the type was correct this time, but not lined up properly – still an obvious fake. Third time was perfect.

Carefully we practiced on two more photocopies, then rolled in the real visa, which had a blue stamp in it. 'Esteli' was typed in. Perfect! The visa looked authentic.

Impressed by my ability to secure a visa on a Sunday afternoon, Craig agreed that I meet him at 7:00 the next morning in front of the hotel.

When the time came, he wasn't there. I found him sulking in the coffee shop. An airport official had called to say that the pilot had had a car accident and another pilot wasn't available. We concluded that this was pure bull and that the truth was that the government didn't want foreigners in the war zone.

Seeing my disappointment, Craig diverted me by sharing some anti-American postcards he'd bought in the hotel's gift shop. On one, a colorful group of peasants was sitting under a tree with books and a teacher; the other side read, 'Many teachers are murdered by the American-backed Contras.' On a second card, two Nicaraguan women were riding a mule; inscribed on the other side – 'The Contras destroy rural transportation with American arms.' A last one showed a picture of a mother in military uniform holding a rifle; her baby was saying, 'Nicaraguan mothers protect their children from American-financed murderers.'

After commiserating about the damaging image these cards gave America, we discussed the Iran-Contra Affair. In an offhand remark Craig mentioned that Khomeini had lived near Paris while he planned the overthrow of the Shah and the

Islamic Revolution. Really? Khomeini was crossing my path again. I filed it away for future reference. Meanwhile, a challenge was at hand – how to get to the rural, Contra-controlled areas without the plane?

Craig had a wife and four children. He seemed to be prepared to let it drop. Not me. Other opportunities existed – to visit the east coast of Nicaragua or some nearby villages – but these weren't important enough to risk exposing the altered visa. So I forged on to my second objective, which was to visit some elementary schools.

When a government, political or religious group is making serious efforts to influence children, the first signs are generally in schools. Art projects, contests, cultural activities and textbooks tend to incorporate subtle or overt messages. In Belfast with schools segregated between Catholic and Protestant, efforts to indoctrinate the children were obvious. Crosses, crucifixes, priests and nuns were prominent in the Catholic schools; Protestant or government schools displayed pictures of Queen Elizabeth and had the Union Jack blowing in the breeze. Textbooks in both slanted political events to favor either the British or Irish nationalist point of new.

Acquiring access to an elementary school in Nicaragua was easier than I'd expected. By avoiding the principal's office and arriving just as classes were ending, I managed not to have to explain my presence or show identification. A bulletin-board display pinpointed where the first grade room was. When a friendly teacher smiled, I introduced myself as a visiting American teacher interested in auditing her class. Between my basic Spanish and her poor English, we could communicate.

The teacher didn't need to explain the art on display. One poster had 'Viva FSLN' in bold black and red letters under the Nicaraguan flag – FSLN, the Sandinista National Liberation Front, was the ruling party. Another showed two children in red and black neck-scarves with 'Niños Sandinistas' printed under their smiling faces. The posters were clearly copied from the Soviet children's Pioneer program. The young teacher, hair pulled back in a ponytail, was indoctrinating her students every day, teaching them how to be good Sandinistas while also instructing them in reading, writing and arithmetic.

I knew from experience how influential a teacher could be. As a senior at San Diego State, I had taken a course from Professor Adrian Kochanski called 'Propaganda and Public Opinion.' While flying as a British pilot at the start of World War II, Kochanski had been shot down by the Germans. The Germans often made Allied prisoners work in factories, and Kochanski was assigned to one of the newspapers run by Joseph Goebbels, Hitler's Minister of Propaganda. Each day he would stride into our class at SDSU holding original German newspapers under an arm. Reaching above the chalkboard, he'd hang them side by side. Translating their texts, he'd trace for us the development and impact of the Nazi propaganda machine. We would be riveted. The man's personal experiences, knowledge of his subject and passion for teaching inspired us to write research papers on controversial subjects involving conflict between the United States and other countries after 1945. The catch was that we always had to argue from the position of the other country. In this way I supported the Soviet Union's version of the U-2 spyplane incident of 1960 in which Francis Gary Powers was shot down over southern Russia. Kochanski's lesson was clear: there are two sides to every story. His further implication was: if possible, go see for yourself. The man's life gave such *gravitas* and substance to his teaching that I'm sure it was partly responsible for my later trips to Belfast, Nicaragua, Cuba, Berlin, Russia, India and of course Paris. Library research provides important background but, through Kochanski, I learned the greater importance of being there.

Only by being in this Nicaraguan classroom was I able to see the bias of the schoolbooks. Only by having their teacher show me the text she used for teaching reading was I able to note that, though it didn't promote anti-Semitism or bigotry, it advocated war and actively acclaimed the Sandinistas. Made up of pictures and simple sentences in Spanish, it was a version of our Dick and Jane; but on the page which showed the letter 'G', the pictures illustrating the sound were of a guerrilla fighter in a ditch with a gun and a military hat – the word 'gorra'. In a more shocking way the math book illustrated the number six by having six military rifles lined up at the top of the page; underneath, two squares had six grenades grouped in twos and threes so that, when added to one another, they equalled six. Of course I had anticipated that the books in use would project favorable images of the government and its struggle to help the people, but I hadn't expected these overtly military images.

Wanting copies of the books to take back to San Diego State, I casually asked the teacher if she needed supplies, such as paper and pencils, which of course she did. Like the clerk at the Intercontinental, she widened her eyes at a twenty-dollar bill I showed, and an exchange was made. Later I learned that it was illegal to take anything out of the country that was considered government property, unless one had proper written permission. The books were duly hidden under my clothes when I got back to the hotel.

What did parents think about these books? In Leon a mother would confide in me that she didn't like the new books and disapproved of the physical education classes too. Along with soccer, children were learning military tactics, such as basic karate, marching in formation while singing military songs, and swimming with fake explosives that could be attached to targets.

My now tattered and dated *New York Times* and *New Yorker* kept generating new friends and invitations. At one party which they got me into, I spotted a female reporter for a major U.S. television network. She was wearing a Sandinista officer's shirt with emblems and rank spread across the front. Very chic for a press party. To me she seemed the jazziest person there, but she apparently didn't think so. Walking up to me, she looked down at my light blue denim shirt with small rhinestones dotting the shoulders and front and said,

'I love your shirt.'

'Would you like to trade?' I asked.

Shortly we were in a small bedroom swapping tops, which delighted us both. When I asked how she'd acquired her shirt, she just smiled and introduced herself as Janet.

My days in Managua showed me that the military and police seemed to have a cordial relationship with the people. They would stand and chat, smoking cigarettes together – very unlike Belfast, where the children threw rocks at the soldiers, or in Mexico, where people crossed the street in order to keep away from the *federales*.

Nicaragua had had a major earthquake in '72, which had destroyed much of the city. As I stumbled through some of the ruins, I found families still living there. Startled, I would step back and apologize for walking into their home, but they'd invite me in and offer coffee. How strange, I mused: here I was, an American from an 'enemy' country and they were offering me hospitality! Frequently I was amazed by this phenomenon: how the people could differentiate person from country. *I* wasn't the problem; America and her policies were. As a thank you, I would take Polaroids and give them to them – it might be their only photo, everything else having been lost in the quake.

During my last week, more photos were taken and more interviews made with parents, students and members of the press who'd been to the border areas – a trip I was never to make. Then three days prior to leaving, while I was sitting in the Intercontinental drinking a beer and waiting for afternoon rains to cease, a young Nicaraguan soldier, soaked to the skin, dashed in holding a bandaged arm.

I offered him a beer. At first he declined, but then he reconsidered and over a brew we chatted in Spanish for thirty minutes about ordinary things, like his brothers and sisters, the nearby military hospital that had tended his arm, his mother and father and how he liked going fishing. At last the rain stopped, and he was gone. But that wasn't the end of it.

When I went into the hotel and ordered a beer the next day, two Nicaraguan men in suits walked up to me and said,

'Miss Mary Duncan, we'd like to talk with you.'

They knew my name and, without asking, sat down.

This was not good. I looked around for a familiar face. No one. Immediately the larger man quietly asked,

'Why did you buy the soldier a beer yesterday?'

'Because it was hot,' I replied. 'He was injured and I was just being nice.'

'What did you talk about?' the smaller one asked in a more authoritative voice.

Clearly on the defensive, I responded, 'Not much. Just his family, brothers and sisters.'

He continued asking what else in a bullying tone. I, who was in a jam, kept responding with the truth. Then I asked who they were. Looking at each other as if deciding whether to answer the question, the smaller man said, 'Internal Security.'

Leaning towards me, the larger man then told me that the soldier had told them a different story. With a sinking heart I realized the innocent soldier was in a lot of trouble, because of my thoughtless generosity.

Thirty tense minutes passed. First the good cop asked a question; then the bad cop hammered me with spy accusations. Finally, when he asked why I'd invited the soldier to my room, which I hadn't, sweat formed on my back.

My room. – Oh my god! My room. In my hotel room I had a Nicaraguan officer's shirt hanging in the closet. Buried in my clothes were the schoolbooks. Meanwhile, in my purse, three feet from their hands, was a forged visa. 'Duncan,' I said to myself, 'you are in deep shit.'

They kept repeating the same questions. Why? What did you

discuss? Who are you, really? What information did you want from him? why invite him to your room? Inferring that I was an American version of Mata Hari almost made me laugh, but the situation wasn't a joke. Visions of being arrested filled my mind, them finding my illegal and suspicious items, me trying to explain to an unsympathetic U.S. consulate officer why I'd done such stupid things. All this heightened my fear. Then the small, combative cop said,

'Please come with us.'

They stood.

This was like a bad movie, except it was happening. Experienced journalists and researchers know how dangerous it can be to get separated from the pack: never let yourself get isolated or arrested without a friend knowing where you are and whom you're with. Again, I looked round. Still no familiar face.

Both of them were standing there waiting for me to get up. Still sitting, I asked them where we were going. Security headquarters, they snapped, the small cop reaching a hand out towards me.

I didn't respond. A smile wasn't going to help. I decided not to leave without a scene. Everyone present would know that I had left unwillingly. Hopefully, that would generate some help now or later.

As I was delaying, preparing to scream if they touched me, I spotted red hair. Thank god, it was Jake, the reporter from Boston. 'Jake,' I yelled. 'Come and join us.'

He strode over, ready for a beer.

I introduced him to the two internal security officers. He got the picture. Making like a hostess, I gestured the two officers to sit back down. But they didn't.

The smaller cop said, 'Miss Duncan your visa expires in two days. We suggest you be on the plane.' – Throwing their shoulders back, the two then walked through the lobby and into the afternoon rain.

Jake looked at me long and hard.

I bought him that beer.

It had been a close call.

For the next two days I stayed out of trouble. Jake and Janet both kept close watch on me until I boarded a Nicaraguan airliner. It wasn't until the plane landed in Mexico City that my blood pressure returned to normal.

11. There Always Was Sex in the City

Back home, Max Lerner and I continued our long-term 'affair'. More and more this caused me to question how he reconciled his intellectual life with his sexual history. At some stage, as I've said, I decided to bring a tape-recorder to our encounters – maybe it was a kind of subconscious riposte to his complaint about the behavior of Kitty Kelly. Whatever, I wasn't wholly prepared for Max's frank and somewhat emotional answers to my queries. Increasingly he opened up to me. The first time I ever heard anyone use the expression 'the conqueror's daughters' was when he revealed the deep anger he'd felt at the social rejection he believed he had suffered as a young, poor student at Yale.

Setting down the yellow tablet he always seemed to have in his hand, he explained, 'When I was there in 1919, there was a girl I used to tutor in Latin. She went to a Catholic convent school and her father was one of the big men in town. I had a score of gentile girls that I played with. Being Jewish and an immigrant, I couldn't really fall in love with a Jewish girl; it had to be the daughter of one of the conquerors.

'She was tall and stately but I'm not sure how intelligent. Nothing ever happened between us, except we used to talk about how we loved each other. She'd go on to say that it was impossible for a rich Catholic girl like her to get involved with a poor Jewish boy. Looking back, I realize it left a scar on me.'

Max described this rejection as entailing 'memories of how my grand Yale classmates, sons of the rich and mighty who rule the world, shut me out of their glittering universe as a cocky, little New Haven yid'. Seducing the daughters of these prominent gentiles became his way of retaliating against the humiliation he had experienced.

Looking towards his desk and room, filled with scattered books and papers, he mused, 'My first sexual liaison was with a young school teacher in Bridgeport, Connecticut. I was a Yale junior. That was the first time I'd ever slept with a girl, and we slept together a great deal. I'd hitch rides into town; she would drive in with her friends. This went on for a couple of years. She wanted to get married, but I didn't see myself married to her. I was in love, but this affair and the ones after never amounted to much – not until Edna. Real love affairs, really passionate romantic love, didn't come until I was teaching at Sarah Lawrence, and then it was more than one at a time.

'At this point I was a young radical, and though I was pretty funny-looking I was sort of romantic. All the girls flocked to me. The president of the college and the deans used to have meetings about what to do about it.'

'You mean they met to discuss your promiscuity?'

'Sure. Finally they decided on a measure that would provide some safety for the girls. In the upper part of each door to a faculty office, they put a little circular window so you could not have complete privacy.'

'Max! Were you actually making it with your students in your office?'

'No. But we would kiss now and then. I want to tell you, Sarah Lawrence was a garden of beautiful girls and I wasn't about to do much resisting.

'I'd see them mostly in hotels. They'd take the train to New York and so would I. That's where I wooed Edna, too. We had a particular hotel in the Times Square area, and I have wonderful memories of us seeing each other whenever we could.'

'How could you afford hotels?'

'O they were cheap in those days [the 1930s]. We used to meet for lunch in the Village and sit and talk. Edna and I did not sleep together so long as she was in college, but I was sleeping with a lot of other girls. Hotels you could rent for an afternoon for something like four dollars. You paid before you went up to your room. That's what they were – brothels, assignation hotels, and everyone used them for this purpose. Anyone who would actually check into one would be crazy, because of all of the noisy fucking all around.

'At one point I had a little room in Greenwich Village in a house where Edna St Vincent Millay used to live. I went there when I was still in my first marriage. Edna and I were intensely in love; she lived nearby with her husband. We'd have assignations, but at one point there was another girl I was also in love with. She was very pretty and also my student at Sarah Lawrence. These were the two Sarah Lawrence girls who meant the most to my life.

'Edna was a great beauty. The other one was also beautiful and very sexually experienced from a young age. She'd lived in Italy and learned sex from all the Italian boys, from which there are no better teachers.'

Being practical I asked, 'What about the transportation problems in New York?'

'Logistics weren't bad.' He laughed. 'I always managed to do it with women who lived in my area. There is a group in New York that lives around Madison Avenue, Fifth Avenue, in what shall we say is a twenty block square. This area is still rife with infidelity and discreet liaisons.

'I got to be known for my promiscuity and the result was that women flocked around me. There's nothing that draws a woman as much as the knowledge that you're going to be faithless to her.'

'That's not true!' I objected.

'Oh, I think it is. They always feel they're going to be the exception.'

'You think so?'

'Sure.' – He grinned.

'I suppose you think that's why they work so hard?'

'That's right. Certainly, it's been my experience. Each woman thinks, "I'm THE ONE!" She knows about the others, but she thinks, "I'm THE ONE!"'

'Well, that says something about you.'

'It says my duplicity is notorious! But she *is* THE ONE when I'm with her. And I feel it. It's not fake. And this is something about love and sex that many people don't know. They don't know the capacity for concentration on a number of partners. The word promiscuity, which I've used a couple of times, isn't meaningful to me. I don't believe there is anything like promiscuity. In other words, variety and promiscuity are not the same.

'I got the word "varietist" from Dreiser [Theodore]. Dreiser called himself a varietist. Gee, I thought when I ran across that, that is just right – I am a varietist. But it doesn't mean I don't have constancy, because I do.'

'Constancy is important?'

'Absolutely! We couldn't have gotten along without it. Fidelity, constancy and continuity are an integral part of my thinking. All three are different from each other. I've had continuity with my wife, for example. We've known each other for fifty years. She's seventy now, and I've known her since she was sixteen, and I fell in love with her when she was sixteen. Now there's continuity in that. And for a time there was passion and for a time constancy, but eventually it became continuity.'

My mind kept mulling over these conversations.

'Max,' I put to him one day, 'Is fucking the conqueror's daughters still the ultimate revenge? Do you deliberately reject Jewish women?'

'No, no,' he said, shaking his head, 'I've certainly fucked and cared about my share of Jewish women. You make me sound anti-Semitic, which of course I'm not. But the old scars run deep, Mary. I'd like to think I've outgrown my anger about how I was treated at Yale, but I haven't. And that was more than sixty years ago.'

'How do you reconcile all of this fucking with your intellectual self?' I repeated. 'Isn't there a conflict when you talk about things like fidelity, constancy, and continuity?'

'I'm writing a book called *Eros in America*. It's not finished yet, but it will deal with these issues. I'm going to dedicate it to Hef. Hef will like that. It will be my way of thanking him publicly for his friendship and generosity towards me.'

Max, who had written twenty-three books, would never complete this one; and I feel privileged to have listened to him expound on the ideas he might have put in it. Often his ruminations to me would appear later in his columns or lectures. I was his audience of one as he organized his thoughts, jotted notes and expressed theories about erotic life in America. *Eros in America* wouldn't have been just another book about sex, he claimed: it would have been a book about the Eros principle as it runs through our lives. – Max felt very strongly about all issues related to Eros, the sexual revolution and love.

'Language is a part of the sexual revolution,' he would say. 'We can't say "fucking", but we all do; and there lies an enormous story. Fucking is most pleasurable, most delightful and most important; but we say "making love". That's peripheral language – talking around it. There are three languages about sex. One is the formal. One is the medical: the body as organism. The third is the street language used between friends, spouses and lovers, if we're lucky. Great literature,' he concluded, 'uses the language of the street.'

He would go on to discuss his eight steps of what he called 'the love cycle':

'At first, lovers are enchanted with one another – enchantment, infatuation, the blush of new love. After this they progress to exploring one another sexually and intellectually – their mutual interests, values and so on. If all is going well, the relationship starts to crystallize and become solid. Commitment is the fourth step; this usually takes place as an engagement, living together or marriage. All relationships have some difficulties then – I refer to this as the "time of troubles"; finances, fidelity, in-laws, religion, career conflicts can all contribute to it. Then comes the period when a couple must "dig to the base" of their love for one another. Is there enough of a foundation for the love to survive? It's at this phase that people will either break up or move on to a new and stronger commitment; it's where they gain new insight and perspective about one another. If they can pass through all that, finally the love will plateau and, hopefully, last as long as mine has with Edna.'

'Max,' I commented, 'your eight steps are good for discussion, but not very practical. Alice di Gesu offers her women friends very practical advice on keeping a man.'

'Really?' he asked. 'How so?'

At the start of the 1980s, Max had introduced me to Alice and her photographer husband, Tony. Alice, who was in her early seventies then, became my guide to tasteful living. She would describe herself as an 'old New York broad', having owned a fashion boutique on Madison Avenue, and was an unfailing, friendly critic of whatever her friends wore. Like Bradley Smith, the di Gesus were old friends of Max from New York. Again, it was an instance of him giving me access to people who would continue to be an influence on my life.

Alice's La Jolla living-room became a salon, consisting of women aged seventeen to seventy. While sipping vodka on the rocks, she would hold forth on the art of keeping a man:

'You must learn and practice the 4-Fs,' she would say. 'The first "F" is obvious. Do it with gusto. He must feel your passion. Whatever he does in bed, you double it.'

I now had Max's full attention:

'Alice said that? And the other "Fs"?' he asked.

Alice was a classic beauty, with high cheekbones and hair swept on top of her head. She almost always dressed in shades of black. Gesturing with her finger, she would continue,

'Flatter your man. Make him feel as if he is the most important creature on this earth. Focus on his positive assets. Don't be fawning; be sincere. If he doesn't have many, dump him. You can do better.'

For those of us who did dump our men or got dumped, Alice was always there to listen and to boost our self-esteem.

When I mentioned that the next 'F' was to feed the man his favorite cuisine, Max laughed and said that at the Mansion that was never necessary: the butlers did it all. Alice however, unlike butlers, who followed orders, advised introducing new foods carefully, interspersed with the man's preferred choices. In this age of diets and cholesterol, she might have added, make an effort to create a healthy lifestyle.

'Men are sensual,' she would stress. 'Appeal to all their senses, with music, food, touching, smelling and seeing. Seeing you, dressed or undressed.'

Nodding, Max harrumphed, 'I have certainly underestimated Alice. All this time I assumed you talked about men, but not with such Machiavellian details.'

'Max,' I countered, 'that's not true!'

'Oh yes it is. And that's probably where the saying comes that "a man chases a woman until she catches him".'

'Max, you'll like the fourth "F".'

'Don't get me wrong. I liked the first three. I've already turned up my hearing aid.'

Freedom was the most difficult concept to comprehend. 'Give a man his freedom,' Alice would say. 'But,' she added, 'Freedom is a two way street. Have your own life. Don't let him ever be too sure of you. Men like a little danger.'

One of Alice's friends added a fifth 'F': create a fantasy and make him the center of it.

'My god, Mary,' Max purred. 'Alice set feminism back a hundred years! I wonder if she realizes she's been teaching what the French courtesans practiced?'

I didn't know. Alice never came to Paris. She died in 2005. She and I talked about her visiting many times; she even got a passport for it. But Alice had a secret that not many people knew: she suffered from agoraphobia. This may explain why she was so welcoming to all and sundry in her home. Occasionally she would venture out to lunch at La Valencia Hotel, shop at a favorite boutique or have drinks at a friend's. But ultimately we brought the world to her.

Max, reaching for his yellow pad, ended our conversation by saying, 'Even if love hurts and leaves bleeding wounds, it's still worthwhile. Always remember that, Mary.'

12. Khomeini in Neauphle-le-Château

Summer had ended. As I resumed teaching, old questions resurfaced from my early trip to Tehran and the Nicaraguan aide worker's comment about Khomeini's exile in France. Just what had he been doing while he was living in that suburb of Paris? I planned a ten-day break at Thanksgiving to go and see for myself.

By now I had developed a travel routine for my various adventures. I would combine an extra week with Easter and Thanksgiving, thus giving me ten to fourteen days of travel twice a year. My students always had excellent guest speakers during my absence. When these jaunts were added to the usual ones I took between semesters, Christmas holidays and summer, my passport was frequently in use. The dean started referring to me as 'professor in absentia'.

Other faculty would occasionally ask how I was able to travel so much when classes were in session. I had my own version of 'don't ask, don't tell'. It was 'don't ask, just go'. I simply completed the travel forms, stated where I was going, for what reason, and when I would return. I usually submitted them only a few days before I left, long after I had purchased my ticket. No one ever objected.

It's important to go through life assuming that what you are doing is OK. My attorney once gave me some wise advice. He said, 'You can ask for permission or you can ask for forgiveness.' I preferred to ask for forgiveness, with a smile. By then I had done whatever it was I wanted to do.

Experience, however, taught me that cooperation was necessary when dealing with some authority figures. My extensive travel caught the notice of the Internal Revenue Service, and it started auditing me. My expenses were high compared to my salary. At first I was annoyed; then I realized it was a game. Instead of me paying them, how much of my tax money could I get them to return?

In addition to receipts, I took copies of my research articles and newspaper stories about my Belfast research to the IRS office. During the audit, I pulled out a list of legitimate items I hadn't claimed. When asked for proof of these expenses, I shrugged, 'Terrorists and informants don't give receipts'. Rattled, the auditor ran off to a supervisor, taking my terrorism articles with him. When he returned, he signed off on my audit.

Sometimes accomplices were needed for skirting university rules. In Paris I had Jim Haynes, the American expat, who taught at a French university. Whenever I wanted to fly to Paris, he would send a fax, letter or email inviting me to lecture to one of his classes. When funds were short, he would let me stay in his guest room or sleep on one of his living-room sofas, which were really twin beds with decorative cushions. Jim's hospitality was such that when I woke up, a stranger was often nearby.

My reasons for flying to Paris varied according to my research interests. For years I had known about Paris' hospitality to exiles, the list including not only literary figures everyone knows of, but also political dissidents, from the Polish nationalists of the 1840s to Communists of the 20th century, such as Lenin and Ho Chi Minh. There were even a few Americans wanted for 1960s upheavals, such as Timothy Leary, doyen of LSD and other drugs, who once fled to France to avoid arrest. Eldridge Cleaver, the Black Panther who had written *Soul on Ice,* fled to Algeria intent to generate support for armed revolution against the U. S. but retreated to Paris to live underground while appealing for political asylum. Residency was granted him in 1974; but after an unsuccessful stint of trying to promote trousers with an outer pouch to show off the penis, he returned to America, served some time and became a fervent Christian.

Margaret Sangar, the birth control advocate, sailed to France in 1913 to avoid arrest for distributing contraception materials in the U.S.. Roman Polanski, the film director, lammed it to Paris in the late 1970s to avoid prosecution in L.A. for sex with a minor. And of course there was Henry Miller and his publishers, prosecuted in the U.S. for pornography as I've said, though never convicted.

Regarding expatriation in Paris, Henry once wrote, 'I was an exile in a foreign country, which in itself gave me a feeling of great freedom.' With this history of welcoming so many figures in flight, it's perhaps not entirely surprising or even necessarily suspicious that France should have allowed the Ayatollah to come live there.

I arrived on a frigid November day. Shortly afterwards, I convinced a French friend to join me in my effort to find Khomeini's home in Neauphle-le-Château.

The train left us outside the picturesque hamlet at a small station. Bundled up against the cold, we walked about half a mile to the edge of town.

'What's the address?' Gilles asked.

'I don't have an address.'

'We came all the way out here and you don't have an address?' he growled.

'Relax. Everyone will know where Khomeini lived.' – And sure enough, the waiter in a brasserie was able to direct us up the winding Route de Chevreuse to Khomeini's house.

It wasn't there anymore. Inside a chain link fence was a pile of bricks and rubble, a bicycle leaning against a tree and a rusted, burned-out car.

Opening the gate, we walked into a large yard to survey this débris. What had happened? Neighbors were looking out their windows at the trespassers, so we decided to introduce ourselves – I should say, I decided to introduce us: Gilles was embarrassed and wanted to flee back to Paris. But he stayed, and after a pleasant exchange with an older man, we asked,

'What about the house?'

'Oh, la la,' the man said, 'In 1982, in the middle of the night, the Shah's supporters blew it up. They hated Khomeini.'

'What did Khomeini do while he was here?'

The old man called his wife over; they talked for a short time. Finally he told us that Khomeini had had three houses: one for his family, one for visitors, a third for staff and supporters. Apparently, the supporters would pitch a blue and white tent in front of the largest house for him to hold prayer meetings in and give lectures to them. According to one newspaper account, he raised over twenty million British pounds in that fashion. The police would barricade the bottom of the street to control traffic. Annoyed with all the visitors, police and reporters, the neighbors were of course glad to see the man leave.

We thanked them and walked back to the ruins. 'Let's go, Mary. It's time for coffee,' Gilles said.

'Just a few minutes. I want to look around more.'

Gilles was impatient. 'If you want a souvenir, take a brick.'

I kicked through the rubble and lifted a few boards. Then I saw some pipes sticking out. Underneath was a broken toilet and the bottom half of a toilet seat. 'I'm taking this,' I said.

'Mary, you can't walk through town with a toilet seat over your arm!' Gilles sighed.

'Oh yes, I can. We'll find a bag in a shop.'

We did find one; and Khomeini's toilet seat hung on the back of the door of my office for many years thereafter, occasionally prompting students to ask questions about him and the Americans who were taken hostage on November 4, 1979 and finally released 444 days later, after contributing to President Carter's defeat and ex-Governor Reagan's election as President. In the meantime, in my research I would make several other discoveries about those events, Khomeini's stay in Paris and my plunder from Neauphle-le Château.

Given the Ayatollah's strict rules on toilet habits, my prize may not have been his own seat; it could well have been one for guests. Khomeini himself is said to have used a hole in an outhouse, where he did not have to face Mecca. An Iranian friend who lived in Paris at the time also told me that the Shah's supporters did not blow up the house; according to him, the French gendarmes blew it up because it was becoming a shrine for Khomeini's followers. A complaint was never filed with the police, and no one investigated the explosion. Neither the town's authorities nor the neighbors could confirm this version of the event and seemed to have forgotten that Khomeini ever existed. A new home has been built on the site.

Some governments at the time felt that France was helping Khomeini as a way to improve access to Iranian oil. Members of the Iranian exile community in Paris believed that there were other contributing factors. One would tell me that the Shah had annoyed the French President of the day, Giscard d'Estaing, by keeping him waiting for fifteen minutes before receiving him at his villa near Montreux, Switzerland. To add injury to insult, at a state dinner the Shah placed Giscard's daughter's fiancé at the end of the table, despite the fact that Giscard had requested he be allowed sit with the family. Giscard, this source told me, had helped Khomeini partly out of spite, not politics. Le Président de la République was not heartless, however. He never sent any Iranian exiles back to Iran after the start of the revolution.

Whatever the truth of such tales, it's generally agreed now that the Shah contributed to his own downfall. When SAVAK, his secret service, offered to assassinate Khomeini for him, he reportedly refused on the grounds that the Ayatollah was a holy man. But regardless of details or who was to blame, Western hospitality surely assisted this man in overthrowing the Shah.

Providing refuge for some kinds of exiles, the ones who aren't relatively harmless literary or political dissidents, can have ambiguous consequences.

13. A Soviet Union

About a year after my pilgrimage to Neauphle-le-Château, I was at a dinner party in La Jolla when Jonathan Freedman, a journalist for *The San Diego Union-Tribune*, mentioned that he had been invited to participate in a human rights conference in Moscow. Looking at me, he added, 'Mary, they need someone with a knowledge of terrorism. Are you interested?'

I didn't hesitate. 'Yes, if you can get me an invitation, I'll go.'

Thus in December 1988, I found myself in snow-covered Moscow with thirty other Americans, each with specific expertise, as guests of the Soviet Peace Committee, a propaganda arm of the Soviet government.

The second evening our hosts had a potluck dinner for our group of citizen diplomats. Because of an interview with Moscow Radio, I arrived late and hungry; all the food was gone except for some desserts. A handsome young Russian, guest of one of the translators, walked up to me and asked if I'd like some cake. People have asked if it was love at first sight. 'No,' I could honestly answer, 'it was lust at first sight.'

The man was Yuri Loskutov. In our intervals of chat over the next few days he told me a fragment of his family history:

His grandmother, Natasha Borisenko, had lived in Odessa. Twice in the 1920s, late at night, a knock had come on her door. Outside in the dark stood a man who said to her, 'Your husband sends love from Paris.' Fearing a KGB ruse, she replied, 'My husband died in a typhus epidemic.' On the second occasion, she added, 'Bring me some proof.' Years later, the man knocked again. This time he handed her her husband Julian's wedding ring, and she wept. By then it was 1938; Stalin had sealed the borders, making travel to and from the Soviet Union virtually impossible. Then the war broke out, and Julian and Mikhail, his younger brother, disappeared entirely, never to be heard from again. Yuri himself only learned about this at his twentieth birthday party: a drunken uncle joked that he might have a rich relation in Paris. Questioning his mother and grandmother, Yuri got first only denial, but after constant badgering the grandmother broke down and told him about Julian. The tale of the typhus epidemic had been to protect the family from Stalin's secret police, seeking supporters of the Czar and their relations. Julian and his brother had been officers in the Czar's army and escaped following the 1917 Revolution via Crimea to Paris.

Before I left Russia, I was appointed co-chair of the Soviet-American Committee on Causes and Prevention of Terrorism. My hosts seriously informed me that I was the most charming CIA spy they'd ever met.

Occasionally after getting home I would call Yuri, since he wasn't allowed to phone out of Russia. The following summer, as I was preparing for my usual trip to Paris, I received a letter from him, forwarded to me by a tourist returning from Moscow. The letter said he was coming to America for six weeks in July. Could he stay with me?

It had been fun in Moscow, for two weeks. But in my home, for six? Yes, I had said that if he were ever in the States, he could stay at my place. But he was a Russian, not an Italian or Frenchman who could travel freely. Frankly, I hadn't expected to see him again.

Checking the calendar, I was relieved to find that I'd be in Paris the first three weeks of his stay. Calling him – a four-hour procedure with an operator – I reluctantly agreed that he could visit after I returned. My biggest question was how had he gotten a visa; later I would learn that two Mormons sent as missionaries to Russia had hired him to be their guide and driver – he could practice his English and earn some money in addition to his job as an architect. After proselytizing this tall, handsome, blond Russian, the Mormons had invited him to Salt Lake City to see their Tabernacle; they had sponsored his visa and paid part of his fare. Yuri, being a bright, enterprising new Russian, had not hesitated either. The rest, as they say, is history.

He arrived on a Greyhound bus wearing a baseball hat with a fertilizer ad on it – gift from one of his new Mormon friends. During his three weeks in Salt Lake City, he had been introduced to several single women; when two had asked him to go on a weekend camping trip with them, he had rubbed his palms together – visions of a *ménage à trois* under the stars. Sadly, he'd been disappointed. All they had wanted was to talk about faith and religion. When I asked how he'd liked Salt Lake City, he replied that the people were nice but that the city was 'more calm than necessary' – in other words, compared to Moscow, it had been boring as hell.

At this time I was still living on the ocean front estate of Dan Dixon. In this romantic setting Yuri and I fell in love. Our marriage, however, was so spontaneous that no one knew we were considering it – even we don't remember the details. We do remember sitting at Villa Surf with friends drinking Margaritas, and I remember suggesting we get married before falling back to sleep. Yuri apparently hesitated before replying that we could get married in Moscow but there was a three-month waiting period. I apparently said that it took three days and a blood test in San Diego, but if we went to Nevada it would only take as long as to find a minister or justice of the peace.

That idea was nixed as soon as I sobered up: it had no class. There was another way, though. California had confidential marriages in some areas of the state, including Lake Tahoe. Designed for people who didn't want the act to be made public for personal reasons – if they had children already and everyone assumed they were already married, for example, or if their children were adult and they didn't want them to know that they were illegitimate – these marriages required no waiting period and only took minutes. In order to qualify you had to say you'd been living together (no one asked how long) and were of legal age, show identification (Yuri's passport would suffice even though written in Russian), pay a fee and be of the opposite sex.

After explaining this to Yuri, I called my travel agent and requested two tickets to Tahoe and a nice room by the lake. Yuri then surprised me by producing champagne and flowers, kneeling on one knee and proposing.

At 2:00 p.m. we boarded United Airlines for a wedding that was out of a situation comedy. The flight was late and we missed our connection in San José. Lake Tahoe was fogged in and we were diverted to Reno, Nevada, from where we were bussed back to Tahoe. The inn wasn't closed, but the wedding chapel was. By then it was 10:30 p.m..

Wandering over to a large hotel, we saw a sign advertising another wedding chapel. It had closed at 8:00, but the manager told us of a further 24-hour chapel outside of town. He called, made an appointment and put us in a taxi. At midnight, we set off to be married Tahoe style.

Yuri of course had no idea how Americans get hitched. In his Moscow people had been married by a judge, not a priest, since the Soviet Union was anti-church; afterwards, you'd visit Lenin's Tomb for luck and have a party.

Snuggling in the back of the taxi, we realized we had no idea of where we were going or who would marry us. Then we pulled up to the chapel, and I was mortified.

Twinkling Christmas lights were strung along the roofline and windows of a small, white, wooden-framed house. A neon sign mounted on the roof proclaimed, '24 Hour Wedding Chapel. Always Open.' Everything needed to be painted, including the white picket fence. But lights were on inside.

Paying the driver, we approached the front door and rang a buzzer. I anticipated some older man wearing a cheap suit; Yuri didn't know what to expect. Neither of us was prepared for the sleepy-eyed, middle-aged, bleached blonde, rumpled and heavy-set, who turned up wearing a dark blue velour robe. The hotel manager had clearly rousted her out of bed.

Yuri was wide-eyed, I embarrassed. The woman invited us in and explained her tariffs. If we used the small tacky chapel to the right, with recorded music, a witness and a Polaroid photo, the price would be $195. The décor of this place actually did a disservice to the word 'tacky': plastic flowers, a rickety altar, metal folding chairs, an old piano and lots of white ribbons hanging from everything... For $150 we could have the chapel, minus the witness. We preferred the least expensive option – $95 to sit in her small office, off to the left, and sign papers making us legal. I was so disconcerted I don't remember if there were any traditional wedding vows.

Wanting to generate a little more revenue, the woman showed us her wedding 'boutique', which had 'Just Married' stickers, garters, more plastic flowers arranged as bridal bouquets, cheap picture frames in case we wanted a Polaroid for posterity. She gave us postcards of the wedding chapel to show to our friends, and Yuri kissed the bride. She called us a taxi, and we drove back to the inn.

Morning arrived – September 7, 1989. I was a Russian bride, and nobody knew it. Basically, Yuri and I had eloped.

After breakfast in the room, we started calling my family and friends. My sister cried for joy amidst her confusion: she and Jim had met and liked Yuri, but wasn't this a little fast? especially given I was clearly not pregnant?

Joyce Gattas, my dean (not the one who had received duty-free liquor) and also a friend, was walking into a morning faculty meeting; her secretary said she would call me later. I replied, 'Tell Joyce I just got married'; within a few seconds she was on the line. 'You did *what*?! Whom did you marry?'

Yuri and I spent two leisurely days in Tahoe, then flew home. A friend called our local paper, which wrote a small article in the local society column; then Yuri flew back to Moscow.

A week later my phone rang. A female FBI agent that I knew said she'd like to come by and interview me.

This wasn't *so* surprising: they'd occasionally interviewed me before about terrorism and my Belfast research. But this time the agent arrived accompanied by a male partner.

I had coffee, they water. After a little conversation she said, 'We read that you've married a Russian.'

'Oh, yes,' I replied. 'We're very happy.'

Looking towards her partner, she asked, 'Mary, this is difficult to put, but has it occurred to you that he might be KGB?'

I laughed. 'Why do you think Yuri's a spy?'

'Well,' she answered, 'he fits the profile.'

'And what is that,' I responded.

'First, he's married a respectable American woman, who is a specialist in terrorism. Second, you live near a major naval base and are on the water, where ships can be monitored and photographed. Third, he's the son of a Soviet general and his mother is a military scientist working for the military. Fourth, he speaks English. Fifth, he can travel outside the Soviet Union. Sixth, he's highly educated, owns a car and lives in housing built for Stalin's high ranking Communist Party members.'

I kept smiling, in order to keep from laughing. 'With that profile, the KGB must think that I'm CIA,' I said.

'Why is that?'

'I've married the respectable son of a general and a military scientist. I travel all over the world and my specialty is terrorism. I'm well-educated and now I've gotten myself appointed to the Soviet-American Committee on Causes and Prevention of Terrorism, which gives me access to high level Soviet experts on terrorism and other aspects of the Soviet military structure. I will also now be travelling to Moscow on a regular basis.'

They looked at each other.

She said, 'We're paid to be paranoid.'

'I understand. But he's no more KGB than I'm CIA.'

This was not the end of the FBI for me.

Two years later, once I'd moved back to La Jolla, my doorbell rang. When I answered, a young woman wearing a dark blue suit showed me her badge and said she'd like to ask me a few questions. Of course, I said, though in the back of my mind I was asking myself why she was alone: usually they travelled in pairs, plus she hadn't called for an appointment. Hmmm, I thought – a green agent.

Before she could say anything else, I sighed and asked, 'Is this about my research with the Irish Republican Army, my Russian husband, my illegal trip to Cuba, my trip to Nicaragua or the prominent Russians I've been bringing to speak at my university?'

She paused, looked at the paper in her hand and said, 'I'm conducting a security clearance on your neighbor.'

I started to laugh.

She looked confused.

The newspaper item that had prompted my earlier FBI visit also brought me a phonecall from the office of a congressman for whom I had once done some *pro bono* work on terrorism. An aide said that they would be happy to assist me in getting Yuri a green card so he could travel to the U.S. freely. 'Thanks,' I replied, 'but I can handle the paperwork.' Chuckling, the aide concluded that I could call him when – not *if* – I ran into problems.

Frankly, Yuri and I hadn't thought that far. A proud Russian, Yuri had had no intention of becoming an American citizen. Still, he didn't want to stand in the lines outside the American embassy in Moscow to get a visa. When I suggested we meet in Paris however, he changed his mind. It would be easier to get a visa to France if he had one for America.

Yuri went off to the embassy while I visited the immigration office in San Diego. What a nightmare! I, who was educated and spoke fluent English, couldn't understand a thing in the forms. Meanwhile, he reported lines wrapped around the block and embassy employees who were rude and unhelpful. I called my congressman's aide. He said he'd facilitate the matter.

When I phoned Yuri the next time, he reported that the embassy had phoned him, told him to come to another door and given him an appointment.

'Mary,' he added, 'I think they have some new employees. They were very nice.'

'No, Yuri,' I said, 'You now have a congressman's name in your file.'

'Ah, so America isn't that different from the Soviet Union.'

I travelled to Moscow that year; then at Christmas in 1990 we met in Paris. Following in his grandfather's footsteps, Yuri came by train. We spent New Year's Eve at Place St Michel, wandered the wintry streets, watched the fireworks and, instead of acting like typical tourists, searched for information at a Russian cemetery and Russian Orthodox churches regarding Julian Borisenko. No luck.

On our last night in Paris, while having dinner with friends, we told them about our search. 'Did you look in the phone book?' one asked. It hadn't occurred to us to do the obvious. Our host thumbed through the directory, found 'M. Borisenko' and called. Speaking in French, he told Mme Borisenko that he was trying to locate relations of Julian Borisenko or Mikhail, his brother. She asked why; he responded that a relation from Moscow was trying to find them. She said she was very ill and hung up. – Fears of the old KGB still haunting her?

The next day we left, knowing we had come one step closer to finding Julian but not having time to pursue it. The matter would have to wait a few months.

I started to spend more time in Moscow, learning how to be a Russian wife, where the rules are quite different. In the early '90s there were still food shortages, though bread, cabbage and potatoes were plentiful, if you were willing to stand in the long lines. Yuri referred to shopping as 'hunting'.

By American standards everything was cheap. Bread was three cents, Coke five, black caviar three dollars a jar. Yuri taught me the first rule of shopping: 'Buy first, think second'. This explained why everyone in his family had the same wallpaper in the living-room: his mother had bought wallpaper for all their apartments when she had found some she liked.

An American wife loves to hear 'buy first, think second', which is the opposite of what an American husband will say. With the rule in mind, seeing some beautiful red floral, cotton quilts in the window of a shop at three dollars apiece, I bought three and took a taxi home. When Yuri opened the door and saw the driver and me with the quilts, he admonished me, saying,

'Mary, we have bedding. Why did you buy these quilts?'

'Yuri, you said to buy first, think second.'

Perplexed, he thought for a moment. Then he asked,

'Was there a line?'

'No, there wasn't even a line.'

With a hopeless look on his face, he explained, 'Rule number two is "If there's not a line, it's not important".'

I regained his respect when I started coming home with hot bread and cooked chickens.

'Where are you getting these?' he asked.

At first I was too embarrassed to tell him for fear he wouldn't approve. From my explorations I knew that not everyone stood in lines. I had observed, for example, that some women walked behind the shops. Following one to a back door, I had seen her knock and another woman answer; the two had talked for a moment, then the second woman had taken some cash and returned with a cooked chicken. The first woman passed on to stop behind a bakery – same procedure. From then on, I did all my 'hunting' by going to back doors. Of course I would pay more, but everything was so inexpensive that it didn't matter. Most of the Russians were charmed by a small American who spoke very little Russian but was good at gesturing and had dollar bills.

One problem perplexed me. Our wooden toilet seat was cracked and I was concerned that I, or a guest, would get pinched while sitting on it. We looked in all the shops and couldn't find any toilet seats. I found myself wishing that I had Khomeini's, still hanging on the door of my office back in San Diego. Then while sightseeing in Tallinn, Estonia, we walked into a department store where on the floor was a pile of plastic toilet seats.

'Yuri,' I yelled across the aisles, 'Toilet seats!' – Quickly I picked up three.

Yuri arrived, embarrassed by my enthusiastic outburst and said, 'We only have one toilet!'

I insisted on buying two.

Yuri's mother Alla and I got along very well – possibly because I didn't speak Russian. She liked that I bought toilet paper in foreign shops and threw away the torn-up newspapers. Alla had been a high-ranking military scientist and worked with Andrei Sakarov, the dissident, father of the Soviet H-bomb. Yuri's father, also a nuclear scientist with a general's rank, had died of cancer caused by radiation poisoning in 1962. Years earlier Khrushchev had assigned him to assist the Chinese with constructing their atom bomb, though after a rift in the late 1950s the Soviet Government withdrew this support. In our livingroom as a result we had silk embroidered tapestries which Mao Tse-tung had given as a thank you to Yuri's father.

Yuri's father's work and rank explained why we had a large, river-view apartment within walking distance of the Kremlin. – In Tahoe I hadn't known I had married so well.

Whenever I stopped in Paris on the way to Moscow I would get Alla a scarf or souvenir. She loved showing these to her neighbors. A sophisticated woman who'd been a part Russia's privileged class, she enjoyed Western fashions. But looking back now, I realize that Yuri and I had made a mistake with her: we had never asked about Julian, her father, or other members of the family. Now it's too late.

Within a year of telephoning the Mme Borisenko who had hung up so quickly, I returned to Paris and, with my artist friend Jill Benjamin, who speaks fluent French, went to the address in the phonebook. The phone had been disconnected; neighbors said the woman had died eight months before, was a widow and had no family. The city had cleared out her public housing apartment. In hopes of finding old photos or letters, we tried to learn where her possessions had gone, but no luck. The trail to find Julian Borisenko ended there. Years later, Yuri and I would continue our search.

Alla, who was now eighty, died suddenly. Yuri called me in La Jolla with the sad news. Yevgeny Yevtushenko, the Russian poet, with whom we'd become friendly, called the Russian consulate in San Francisco and got me an emergency visa. As I flew off to Moscow, I didn't know what to expect.

The night prior to the funeral, two women friends came to our flat and started to cook in the kitchen. The dining-room table was expanded to seat over twenty people – by now I was used to Yuri's creative arrangements: since we didn't own twenty chairs, he put two bed slats in between two chairs, covered them with blankets and thus created benches.

Next morning the guests arrived, along with a rented school bus to take us to the mortuary and crematorium.

The mortuary was a small, plain, gray, concrete building surrounded by fresh snow. Alla was laid in a beautiful open casket with red satin lining, symbolizing her country. There were no religious symbols in the room; above her head was a red satin pillow filled with the medals the Soviet Union had awarded her for many years of service. Approximately thirty people stood around, each holding an even number of flowers. One by one, they recalled their friendship with Alla and, as they spoke, lay a flower on her chest. Within half an hour, Alla and the casket were overflowing with colorful roses, carnations and lilies.

We walked back to the school bus. The rear door opened

and Alla's casket was slid in on two metal tracks, then clamped down. The seats faced inward, so we all sat around her facing the casket on the ride to the crematorium.

Unlike the mortuary, the crematorium was a large, impressive, marble building, surrounded by a parking-lot filled with cars and other mortuary school buses. Like the other mourners, we had an appointment.

Before we entered, Alla's casket was rolled out and put on a conveyer belt. Once inside, this led on to a draped opening in the wall. Numerous other people were already there standing beside their loved ones, along another long wall.

Alla's casket was opened. A small woman in a black dress asked if anyone would like to say anything else about her. Several did, and more flowers were placed on her chest. At last the woman turned to Yuri and asked quietly if his mother had been baptized; he nodded yes. Crossing herself, she said a quiet prayer; then the casket was closed and a button pushed. As it moved before us towards the draped opening in the wall, people placed their hands on it in final farewell. Alla was cremated as we stood holding hands. She died never knowing what had happened to her father after he had fled to Paris.

Back at the apartment, the women hung a large photo of Alla in the entry. A delicious dinner was prepared for family and guests. Drinking, eating and salutations to Alla carried on through the night.

I will never forget this Russian-style funeral and how everyone participated in Alla's farewell to our world.

We have much to learn about how to bury our loved ones.

14. In Simone de Beauvoir's Apartment

A timely arrival from Moscow to Paris landed me in Simone de Beauvoir's apartment at 11 bis Rue Schoelcher. There were masks on the walls and sofas on which famous people had sat. Books lined the shelves, and a large pile of them sat in the center of the floor. These are what had brought George Whitman, current owner of Shakespeare and Company, to the apartment.

George had been contacted by Sylvie le Bon de Beauvoir, Simone's adopted daughter, who wanted to sell her mother's English language library. I had arrived at the Shakespeare and Company shop that wintry morning as George was preparing to set out to inspect the collection. When he told me why he was so buoyant, I instantly asked if I could go along and help carry whatever he bought.

As an hour dragged on, I sensed that something might upset the expedition. Sure enough, as George and I got on a bus toting large canvas book bags, he said, 'Can't find her address, must be here somewhere...' As he rummaged in his pockets, my heart sank. How could anyone misplace *her* address? Those of us who knew George knew it was a real possibility. Rummaging some more, he had no luck. However, he did remember the street name and that it was a short street. I sighed with relief.

'George, Simone was famous. Someone on that street will know where she lived.'

Fortunately, the second older woman we asked could point out de Beauvoir's building.

It was in a white Deco structure facing the ivy-covered walls of the Montparnasse Cemetery. It had large high windows and wrought-iron and glass doors, which opened into a courtyard.

De Beauvoir's apartment was five steps up to one side, through another set of double doors. Sylvie must have been watching for us, because she came out before we could ring a buzzer.

Wearing a dark blue sweater and loose-fitting pants, she looked a little dishevelled, probably from fussing with books. Her long dark hair was swept behind the ears; red shoes added a flash of color.

As she led us up and in, I absorbed the historic atmosphere. George knelt on the floor to peer into the volumes. Agreeing a price on the spot, he paid her, in cash. Incredibly – I don't remember why – I had a video camera with me and so could photograph the entire event.

Per George's instructions, we started to place two to three hundred of de Beauvoir books into his bags. To add festivity to the event, also not wanting to appear intrusive, I asked Sylvie if she'd like to look through the lens of my camera. She took it and focused on George, sitting on the floor next to the pile.

'Video me with him,' I said, but, not being familiar with the apparatus, she fumbled. I had show her how to use the forward and back buttons.

Looking steadily through the lens, she asked, 'Why do you wish to take these pictures?'

I was afraid she'd stop. 'Simone de Beauvoir's library is a part of history,' I blustered.

'Yes, yes,' she responded.

'Here I am collecting her books, and I thought I was just going to come and have tea with George!... I'm an admirer of your mother's. I learned a great deal from her.'

This was not just flattery to prevent her from stopping filming. As I've mentioned, it was especially the concept of 'alterity' or the 'other' discussed in *The Second Sex* that had long ago impressed me. De Beauvoir had understood early on the problems related to women living their lives as an extension of somebody else, rather than for themselves. Coming from an upper middle-class family, she had also known that economic independence is key to a woman's independence. Ultimately, her writing had led her to financial solvency. It was with the prize money from the Prix Goncourt, which she won for her novel *The Mandarins*, that she had bought this apartment, in 1955.

These thoughts distracted me while George barked out a warning to be careful with his new books. Handing over the camera, Sylvie took my place. With George's craggy features in the lens, my reverie now moved on to what he had once told me when I'd asked him what motivated him:

'Inertia,' he'd replied, roving around his shop. 'You throw a stone, just as Spinoza said, and it goes in that direction because it wants to.... I believe in determinism. I don't believe that we are living but we are being lived by cosmic forces. I have a tragic sense of life...'

As he sorted books, handling them with infinite care, it was hard for me to believe that George had a tragic sense of life. Books give us life, and his love of them and desire for his shop to go on and on clearly motivated him to keep living. – At this time he was already nearly eighty.

While they filled bags, I panned the living room. It had an international flair. Ethnic fabrics, primitive dolls, small statues, faded brightly-colored satin pillows mixed with brown pillows lined the walls behind the sofas that stood in the corners – really twin beds. Because of the pile of books, Sylvie had moved two small satin-covered chairs, one white and the other purple, close to the ends of the sofas. Perched on the edge of a bookshelf above were two bottles, of vodka and vermouth. Long red drapes covered tall windows above the shelves; they were closed, but identical ones across from the sofas were open, letting soft winter light filter in through sheer curtains. The room differed little from how it looked in a famous shot of it by Jacques Pavlovsky, the French photographer. Instead of a light-colored fabric, two American Indian blankets were now tucked around the mattresses, one white with a brown design, the other red with a black and white design. Gone was the dark wooden, rectangular coffee table with its drum and vase of flowers; in its place was a low, round modern one holding a telephone.

Simone de Beauvoir had created a lovely sitting area for herself, Sartre and their friends, even if the Deco building lacked some of the old world charm of others down the street. The kitchen was small, functional and looked as if it didn't get much use – an empty drainer, a bunch of towels on a hook and a pasta poster on the wall over the sink. But everywhere the apartment had the most important feature: the aura of its one-time possessor.

As bags continued to fill, I noticed several copies of *The Mandarins* and *Force of Circumstances,* books that had caused a breach in Simone's relations with the American novelist, Nelson Algren, author of *The Man with the Golden Arm,* who had felt that she betrayed their intimacy. Several paper, hardback and leatherbound copies of *The Second Sex* were also visible through the dust. Did the small metal spiral staircase between the living-room and kitchen lead to her bedroom. What was it like? – Not wanting to press my luck, I didn't ask. Meanwhile, I wondered, why was Sylvie selling her mother's English language books to George? Had she offered them to other bookstores or libraries first? And what was in the other boxes that she moved to a far area of the room while George filled more bags? Was there something she wanted to keep from him?

Personal questions about Simone surfaced, such as who had visited her and slept here? Did it include Sartre? other lovers? Algren? Claude Lanzmann? What had Simone's relationship been with Sylvie, and why had she adopted an adult female?

Some of these questions would be answered later. Meanwhile, helping George again, I got Sylvie to speak...

Her mother had been compulsive and wrote wherever she happened to be – in this apartment, in Sartre's flat, at Café Flore, friend's homes and the hotels they went to on vacation. Pausing thoughtfully, Sylvie said that she missed reading Simone's manuscripts before they were published. And Sartre *had* spent a lot of time in this apartment, I would learn. 'I rise at eight-thirty in the morning,' he had told an interviewer for *The New York Review of Books*. 'Often I sleep at Simone de Beauvoir's house and have breakfast in a café on the way home.' He would work in his apartment until afternoon, when Simone would arrive – in *Tête à Tête,* Hazel Rowley notes that he was frequently grouchy in the morning. They would talk; Simone would read to him; then they would go back to her apartment around nine. According to Sartre, they would listen to music, then she would read to him again and he'd go to bed a little past midnight.

Perhaps the bed he was talking about was in the sleeping loft, up those spiral steps? the area I couldn't see into?

After two hours, bags full, George asked Sylvie to call us a large taxi. Waiting for it, which took some time, I scanned the room a final time. It felt sad now, with those gaps on the partly empty bookshelves.

We sat on the sofas with the large pillows behind us while Sylvie spoke softly about how her mother had spent many hours entertaining friends and colleagues here. Referring to her death in April 1986, she murmured, 'The operation wasn't necessary. I miss her everyday.'

Simone de Beauvoir had died suddenly in hospital a couple of weeks following surgery. Exploration had shown that she had cirrhosis of some internal organs and pulmonary edema. In April, 1980 Sartre had died of similar illnesses.

Sylvie walked us to the cab and held its doors open as we awkwardly placed bags on the back seat. Saying *au revoir*, we rode off to Shakespeare and Company to sort through these treasures. Before we arrived, George attempted to answer some of my further questions:

Complex French inheritance laws had persuaded Simone to adopt Sylvie so she would have an heir. Without an heir, the government would have acquired a sizable amount of her estate. French law favors family members; Sartre had adopted Arlette Elkhaim for the same reason. It was because Sylvie was heir that she had the right to sell the library. George concluded that she'd approached him rather than some institution because Simone had occasionally stopped by his stop in its early days.

'Simone used to live on Rue de la Bûcherie,' he explained. 'Same street.'

She had moved into a flat at 11 rue de la Bûcherie in October 1948. Located on the far side of Park Viviani from Shakespeare and Co, it had three rooms on a top floor, with a view of Notre Dame, a leaky roof and no bath. While there, Simone had published *The Second Sex* and *The Mandarins*. There too she and Nelson Algren had been lovers. She had promised him that 'this will be our place' and 'no man but you will ever sleep here', but she broke the promise in 1952 when she became lovers with Claude Lanzmann, then a young journalist.

Number 11 rue de la Bûcherie no longer exists. Simone's doorway is incorporated into the four-star Colbert Hotel, whose main entrance is around the corner at 7 rue Hotel Colbert. The noisy, dark Algerian restaurant whose music Algren complained about has been gone for years; instead of the weird, ancestral staircase that Algren describes, the Colbert has installed an elevator, though stairs are still necessary to reach the top floor. Nor can Rue de la Bûcherie any longer be described as an area with tenement housing. Fashionable art galleries, restaurants and boutiques line the street.

I would visit Simone's former apartment eventually. It is now called the Superior Suite. Walls are covered in pale blue paper; dark blue and gold carpeting covers the floor and bright pink marble adorns the bathroom. I wonder if Algren would have approved? Both scribes would probably have liked a small writing desk near the window overlooking Notre Dame. But conspicuously absent are the dozens of books they would have had lining the walls.

The cab driver helped us carry in George's book bags. George placed them first on the floor of the bookstore alongside the front desk, but after a few minutes he decided that there was more room in his antiquarian library next door. Not wanting the sensation of being so close to Simone de Beauvoir to end, I volunteered to sort the contents. Probably pleased to have someone organize this maze of literary history, George agreed. So, with Notre Dame in the background, tourists wandering by the windows, a partially made bed used by one of George's young students to one side and hundreds of books lining the walls, I began the pleasant task of sorting a Simone library anew.

After a brief survey, I began making five stacks on the floor and table. The first contained books written and signed by Simone, including bright red leather volumes of *The Second Sex*. Second came unsigned books. Works by Sartre constituted a third, smaller group. Fourth came miscellany. The fifth and final pile was possibly the most fascinating: books sent to Simone and inscribed to her by other famous authors.

My own selection narrowed down to five of the inscribed books, plus two unsigned paperbacks of *The Second Sex*. I paid George $125 for them. Later I would send a friend a copy of *The Second Sex*, telling her that though it was unsigned, George Whitman and I had personally transported it from Simone de Beauvoir's apartment.

Curiosity and respect for Upton Sinclair led me to select *A Cup of Fury*, a book warning about the negative affects of alcohol on creative people. The inscription simply read, 'To Simone de Beauvoir. With best wishes. Upton Sinclair.' I wondered whether Sinclair knew how appropriate his choice of book was. De Beauvoir's and Sartre's deaths were both hastened by alcohol.

Gloria Steinem, a great admirer of de Beauvoir, had signed *Outrageous Acts and Everyday Rebellions* 'For Simone de Beauvoir. A member of the international feminist government in exile – and my much-loved sister. With respect, Gloria Steinem. 12-16-83.' I don't know if she ever met Simone or how Simone felt about her, but Steinem was definitely grateful for the path this predecessor had paved for her and other women. So I took her book.

Another feminist who knew de Beauvoir well, Kate Millet, travelled with her and Sylvie in the summer of '83 through New England and New York State. According to one biographer, Sylvie planned this vacation to help Simone recover from an illness and the deaths of Algren and Sartre. During the trip they'd stayed at Millet's farm in Poughkeepsie, which apparently functioned as a feminist, communal art colony – it would be cited by Simone 'as a possible model for feminist life in France'. Millet signed her book, *Sexual Politics*, 'For Simone de Beauvoir with great admiration from one of those who followed afterward – With kindness and wisdom, Kate Millet.' I took that one too.

The fourth book I took, *America As A Civilization*, had been sent to Sartre by Max Lerner. I could hardly pass it up. Max had inscribed it, 'For Sartre in friendship per Algren.' Later Max would tell me that he'd sent the book in 1960 via his good friend Nelson Algren when he'd learned that Algren was travelling to Paris to visit Simone.

The last book I took also related to Algren. When he and Simone had still been close, he had sent her *The Story of An African Farm* by Olive Schreiner. Inside, he had written: 'For Simone. In hope of seeing her city and her, one day again. As ever, Nelson. May 1, 56.'

Nelson Algren did see the apartment again. On that 1960 trip to Paris, which turned out to be his last, he had stayed there. And when Simone died, she would be wearing a ring he had given her. But she would be buried next to Sartre, in the Montparnasse Cemetery.

While I was sorting books, a young man who was staying in the bookstore wandered in and asked what I was doing. After telling him, I asked if he knew why George referred to him as a 'tumbleweed'. He didn't.

Somewhere along the line, George had nicknamed his establishment 'The Tumbleweed Hotel' in honor of the dozens of hippies who'd come through the place, some on trips between Paris, Kathmandu and, say, Bali, making jewellery and living by their wits. George looked at these characters as tumbleweeds. But the real impetus for him providing a 'hotel' was to return the generosity he felt that poor people had shown him when he'd travelled in South America as a young man. He'd been returning this favor even since he'd opened the store in August 1951. In payment for a bed, the 'tumbleweeds' would be expected to spend a couple of hours sweeping floors, shelving books or washing windows. One task puzzled me: why would anyone want to put perpetually broke students or other drifters short of cash in charge of the moneybox? – George did, on a regular basis.

As night fell over Paris, Simone de Beauvoir's apartment, the Seine and Shakespeare and Company, I continued my sorting. Taking a break, I walked out and washed the dust off my hands in the dark green, Wallace drinking fountain with four maidens holding its dome; then I went back to grouping books. Afraid to stop even to eat for fear that someone else might take over, I finally completed the job around midnight. Physically tired but mentally exhilarated, half in the past and half in the future, I walked back to a friend's apartment.

Next day a handmade sign appeared in Shakespeare and Co.'s window: large black and green letters proclaimed in three lines 'Books from the Library of Simone de Beauvoir and J. P. Sartre'. Over the next few weeks, people came and bought the collection, though George kept many books for the shop's own library. My own five volumes now sit on a shelf in my Paris living-room, not far from Simone's apartment. George is ninety-three as I write; he still tells the students who stay at his shop to read a book a day and travel the world while they're young and once again when they're old. Thanks to him, many of the English language books from de Beauvoir's library now live in the homes of her admirers. We possess something this great woman of our times once held and cared for.

15. Shakespeare and Company: Moscow Style

The experience of being in Simone de Beauvoir's apartment and helping to organize her collection of books accelerated the angst I felt in Moscow in the early '90s. Lack of modern conveniences like hot water in the summer months, long food lines and using torn newspapers for toilet paper didn't particularly bother me. The shortage of English language books did.

When I'd started living in Moscow several months a year, the city had only one English language bookstore. It was overpriced and had rude, unhelpful clerks who didn't speak English. The majority of books were classics, dictionaries and outdated British editions. I yearned for a store similar to Shakespeare and Company in Paris where you could browse, spend Sunday afternoons drinking tea and Monday evenings listening to writers reading their poetry or discussing new books.

Before the collapse of the Soviet Union in 1991, most Russian bookstores were still owned and subsidized by the government, as were most other shops. A few had some used English language books which tourists had sold to them, but finding them was like mining for diamonds. You weren't allowed to touch books; they were sequestered on shelves behind counters or in glass cabinets. You had to point to what you wanted; the clerk would then hand it to you and linger to make sure you didn't steal it. Not a very enticing consumer experience.

The books were cheap – ten cents for a used copy of Hemingway's *The Old Man and the Sea* or of Mark Twain's *Tom Sawyer* – but those who wanted books other than 'classics' had to lug them in suitcases competing for space with everything else we Westerners felt we needed to bring there. When Yuri and

I would plan a dinner party, I'd ask the guests to bring English-language books to exchange. If they brought three, they could take three. They ended up being more interested in swapping books than in eating and drinking.

One fateful evening in December 1992, I decided to open a Shakespeare and Company in Moscow. No doubt this dream had started back in the Writer's Room of Shakespeare and Co. in Paris. In the 1980s George had put me there whenever I needed a place to stay; for me it was the most intellectually seductive spot on earth. Located on the first floor above the shop, it overlooked the Seine and Notre Dame. The famous cathedral's bells would wake you, reminding you that you were in a magical place. Hundreds of books lined the walls, reflected in a large gilded mirror hanging at the end of the 150 square foot space. An old desk rested under the window, cluttered with George's invoices, unanswered correspondence, a dried-out coffee mug. In a tiny nook stood a sink, which had running water. An old toilet was out in the hall, but like many of George's residents who slept on beds nestled between bookshelves I kept coins for the 'loo at the corner café. One of the best-kept secrets in Paris was the public bath on the Île St Louis where for about one dollar you could have a towel and use of a very clean, private shower.

On Sundays at four when tea was served in George's upstairs apartment, the late Ted Joans would regale groups of rapt listeners crammed into a small back bedroom with the story of Shakespeare and Company. Pointing to a photograph of Sylvia Beach, he would explain how she'd founded the original store in 1919 on rue Odéon with the help of Adrienne Monnier, who became her lover. Sometimes a young innocent would be visibly shocked by this disclosure. 'Oh yes,' Ted would say, waving his long arms towards a wall full of photos. 'Many famous people came to Shakespeare and Company... It was the Nazis in World War II that forced Sylvia to close it down.'

I lived on ham and cheese baguettes, inexpensive wine, George's pancakes and strong tea. I wish I could say that I did a lot of writing then, but I didn't. Instead I did a lot of dreaming – dreaming of living and writing in Paris: the cliché that everyone around Shakespeare and Co. lived by.

My fondness for the place grew each time I visited. Greeting me, George would immediately insist that I read a new book; he didn't care if I bought it or not. Sometimes his young daughter, Sylvia, might be chatting with customers or helping serve tea. When I told George, in early 1993, that I wanted to open a Shakespeare and Company in Moscow, he was visibly thrilled.

I'd never had a business. My experience was limited to selling Girl Scout cookies, with mixed success depending on whom you spoke to.

I started by hiring a translator and visiting all the bookstores in Moscow, my strategy being to find a partner who already had a shop and expand it to include English language books. I also started buying boxes of used books and bringing them back to the Moscow apartment.

Yuri was not amused – he felt that our furnishings should consist of more than cartons of dusty books.

While on a cruise to St Petersburg, I scoured all the river cities looking for dual language books in English and Russian. We acquired piles of books, but no bookstore. As usual, like in Belfast, I was going in cold.

When I returned to Paris, George informed me that he was going to bring some boxes of books to Moscow as a present for my new store. Proudly, he showed me where he had added 'Moscow' to a list of cities on his sign. My God, what had I done? How could I tell him I didn't have a partner or a location?

Back in Moscow, two things happened which I took as favorable omens. First, while browsing in a metro kiosk, Yuri spotted a stack of *Tropic of Cancer* paperbacks in Russian (translation most likely pirated) at a cost of fifteen cents each. I bought twenty copies and later gave two to George. Henry Miller would be one of the first authors to line our shop shelves.

Second, as a trial run, I had four boxes of used books sent by ship from San Diego to Moscow. Four months later a small canvas bag was delivered with only five books in it. At first I was depressed – almost all the books had been stolen – but sifting through the remainder, I proudly showed Yuri that Adrienne Monnier's biography had made it through. Since Adrienne had encouraged Sylvia to open Shakespeare and Company in the first place, I decided to forget about the loss of the other books and take this as a sign of luck.

In the summer of 1993, George arrived by train with a female college student and four boxes of new books. When we met them at the station, Yuri's eyes got wide at the sight of more books, but graciously he carried the heavy boxes to our car. George was so pleased to see all the boxes in our hallway that even Yuri laughed. Now I *had* to open the bookstore. I'd lose too much face with George if I didn't.

In between teaching and trips to Paris and Moscow, I kept researching how to run a book shop. Dennis Wills, owner of D. G. Wills Books in La Jolla, taught me about distributors such as Ingrams and advised me not to buy anthologies, to stock paperbacks whenever possible, to give credits for used books and to let the customers spend the credits in the store for more books. His final advice was to give cash for books only when all else failed.

Other role models included Warwick's Bookstore in La Jolla, which, similar to The Village Voice in Paris, offered a more upscale approach: wine at readings, books placed tidily on the shelves, credit cards accepted and customers able to order books not in the shop. D. G. Wills and Shakespeare and Co. were a little more laid back. But both stores now accept credit cards, and Shakespeare has new carpeting, wiring and a cash register.

After a year of scouring Moscow, I finally found a partner – Alexander Ivanov, 'Sasha', referred to me by another shop owner. My translator arranged for us to meet at his small store near Paveletskaya metro station, close to the city center.

As we walked down into a basement, we saw customers browsing along tables and shelves. Sasha was seated in a small alcove waiting to serve tea. In fluent English he introduced us to his wife, Lena.

I'd prepared a talk explaining the concept of establishing a literary store like the famous Shakespeare and Company in Paris. As I started, Lena interrupted, 'We know all about Shakespeare and Company. I'm a Gertrude Stein scholar at my institute. We've visited the Paris shop.'

We hit the ground running. Mutual enthusiasm spilled over into the shop. Customers kept looking at us to see what the merriment was about.

'Sasha,' I said, 'You have a wonderful place here, but there's no room for English language books.'

'Oh Mary, we have lots of space. Come: I'll show you.'

We walked out and around to the other side of the tall, modern, sixteen story apartment block. Sasha led the way down concrete steps into another basement.

A bare light bulb hung from the center of a low, six-foot-ceilinged room. An old man sat on a rickety cot surrounded by empty vodka bottles. Large water roaches crawled in and out of small puddles on the uneven dirt floor; rat droppings were everywhere; a small adjoining room had mounds of dirt and more signs of rodent life.

Before I could run out the door, Sasha introduced us to Alexei, who clearly had a drinking problem. 'Alexei is our watchman,' he winked. Then he started pointing to where shelves could be built in the 600 square feet of space.

'Sasha,' I asked, 'Do you really believe a bookstore could be created here?'

'Absolutely! My basement was worse than this before we started renovating it.'

We wrote out a contract, which was really a signed handshake. I knew that an American wouldn't stand a chance in a Russian court against a Russian citizen – when investing in Russia, only invest what you can afford to lose was a common saying among potential investors. We each contributed $6500 towards creating Shakespeare and Company, Moscow. Sasha, who understood how to get things done, would be responsible for the workers and design of the shop; I would be in charge of supplying the books and publicity. We had no budget for books.

Progress was slow. The apartment owners would not let us use noisy electrical equipment, so all the dirt, rocks and débris had to be dug out by hand. Still, slowly things began to take shape. Each time I returned to Moscow, Yuri would drive me by the store before going to our apartment. Alexei, our 'watchman', disappeared. Sasha explained that the space had become too gentrified for him.

On every flight into Moscow, I would bring some 200 pounds of used and new books with me. Stacked in suitcases, they would push Delta's luggage limits to the max. At first Russian customs was not a problem; then they initiated a rule that passengers were to be charged per pound for any luggage over 100 pounds. I vowed not to pay.

Baggage porters got to know me because I tipped well. I told them in my poor Russian that if I didn't have to pay any customs fees, I would give them $20. They'd try to steer me to a friendly customs officer. When that didn't work, I would play dumb. Once they weighed my bags and told me in broken English that I owed over $200 dollars, I would ask why. They would explain, but I would deliberately not understand. A senior customs officer, who spoke better English, would eventually arrive; meanwhile, the line behind me would have grown very long and people were grumbling.

He would explain again. I would shrug and say,

'These are used books. They're not worth $200 dollars. Keep them and read them with your tea.'

In reality, the books could be worth as much as $1500.

In exasperation, he would eventually wave me through.

I never paid one dollar for customs duties.

Yuri said I had acquired the skills of the old Russian babushkas known for their abilities to frustrate and defeat bureaucrats.

In early 1996, three months before our opening, Sasha had bad news. A large, new English language bookstore had opened in the center of Moscow. Its location was better, with good street access. It had beautiful high ceilings and had hired an experienced American manager.

Of course I went instantly to inspect this competition. It turned out worse than I had imagined – they were also going to open a large café.

I decided to introduce myself to the new manager and be honest about who I was. We liked one another. She was frank about their shipping problems, which had increased their costs, and some small difficulties with the local mafia. For some reason I wasn't demoralized. Somehow I knew things would work out. Sasha laughed at my American optimism but agreed we'd come to far to quit.

We decided to open on April Fool's Day, because everyone said we were fools. You'll lose your money; the mafia will run you out of business; customers will steal from you; your Russian partner will cheat you, etc.. Two weeks before the opening party, our shelves were only twenty-five percent filled. Then the phone rang. The manager of the other bookstore was on the line; she announced they were closing in three days. A neighboring restaurant and the local mafia had created major problems, and the New York owners had decided that without a café the store wasn't worth investing in. She suggested I call one of the owners, who was in Moscow, and make an offer for their stock.

'But we don't have the money for all your new books, even with a big discount.'

'If he doesn't sell them, he's going to have to ship them back to New York, which would be expensive and a logistical nightmare. Offer to buy them on consignment at thirty percent of retail. Pay for them as you sell them.'

I called. He said yes. Two days later his staff delivered $30,000 worth of books to our door.

Sasha became a believer.

Yuri painted a large sign with the head of Shakespeare on it, similar to the one at Shakespeare and Co. in Paris; we hung it and celebrated with a bottle of champagne. Yuri of course had another reason to celebrate – our apartment was no longer cluttered with boxes of books.

Sasha had our electrician install modern, high wattage ceiling lights, since we only had one small window and a doorway for natural light. With a Californian's concern about electricity bills, I tactfully asked the cost.

'It is of no concern,' he said. 'It doesn't matter how much electricity we use.'

I didn't understand. 'Sasha, we have a meter.'

'The meter is only for decoration – relax! In Russia people are billed by how many square feet or meters of space they have, not how much electricity they use. If we burn candles, the bill will be the same.'

Oh, how I wished it were the case in San Diego!

On March 31, 1996, we had our opening party. Diplomats from the American, French, Israeli, Indonesian, Swiss and British embassies crowded our small space, along with Russian writers, friends, neighbors and reporters from the Moscow *Times* and *Tribune*.

Our excited guests caught us off-guard. As wine, vodka, juice and Coca-Cola flowed, they started buying books. As salami, bread, cheese and fruit were gobbled down, we improvised and asked one of our new staff to set-up a moneybox.

After the first week, we were a financial success. Of course our overheads were low. The staff, which was bilingual, was paid $1 an hour – a good wage then. Sasha, who was a shrewd businessman, had negotiated an inexpensive twenty-year lease with the building. Our daily outgoings were $18, including salaries, rent and utilities.

We had to teach our young Russians to smile and be helpful with customers. The problem was helped when we hired Sarah and Jennifer Flugge, two missionaries' daughters. We told the others to follow what the Flugges did; still, they would only be polite with Western customers, ignoring their fellow Russians, claiming that they didn't expect smiles or good service. Eventually, after much coaching, we had everyone receiving American 'service with a smile'.

One of our Russian staff, Ira Okuneva, was taking French lessons and would study when business was slow. At the time, because of visa restrictions and money, there was little hope of her ever visiting France, yet she continued on with her studies. 'Even if I never travel to France', she said, 'learning a language is a valuable intellectual experience.' This taught me a lesson: through initiative and perseverance, Ira finally received a grant and now lives and works in Paris.

During our first week, a dapper, middle-aged Russian came in and bought over a hundred dollars worth of books. His favorite writers were Kurt Vonnegut and John Fowles. He asked if we'd had any visitors requesting payments for protection services, a quaint way of referring to the local mafia, also known as 'krisha' or 'roof'. When I said no, he handed me several business cards, which identified him as the director of a Russian bank. He told me to give one to anybody who bothered us and have them call him. Eventually we gave out three, and that ended our problems with local gangsters. Our friendly protector visited a couple of times a month and always bought an armful of books.

Even though our store was on a small street without a lot of foot traffic, business thrived. Newspaper stories and the current books I kept bringing over in my suitcase helped. U. S. embassy wives would take fliers and distribute them at embassy events and meetings. We had a small refrigerator in our adjoining lounge that was always filled with wine, vodka and Coca-Cola; given the relaxed or non-existent liquor laws, we soon became known as the world's only bookstore where you could get tipsy as you browsed. At Christmastime I upped the ante, introducing our customers to Mexican coffee, which we mixed with tequila, Kahlua and whipped cream. The cost of the drinks was more than paid for by our increase in sales.

One day I nearly tripped over an old woman crouched behind our large center table. 'Excuse me!' I blurted. She quickly shushed me, putting a finger across her mouth and motioning me to kneel down beside her. In a frightened voice she said, 'The KGB is after me. Don't tell them I'm here.'

No one else was in the shop; but when I mentioned the matter to Sasha later, he laughed and told me that having a crazy customer was considered to be good luck. 'Don't scare her away or we'll have a spell cast on us.'

Saturday nights became cultural events. Cigarette in hand, Sasha would be a charming host. Through his and our contacts, many of Russia's leading writers and poets came to read at small, but lively salons: Victor Erofeyev, Yevgeny Yevtushenko, Vladimir Sorokin, Tatiana Tolstoya, Lev Rubenstein, Dimitri Prigov and others. Sylvia Beach might have been proud.

Our efforts did not go unnoticed by the diplomatic corps. One afternoon a U.S. embassy staff person walked in and handed me an envelope; inside was an embossed invitation to a reception at the ambassador's residence. From then on Sasha and I along with our spouses were invited to receptions at Spasso House, a gesture duly appreciated.

If theft was a problem, we were not aware of it. In fact, one customer tried to return a book. She came into the store holding her tearful six-year old son by one hand; in the other, was one of our children's books. In broken English she said, 'Dimitri took your book and he is returning it.' She nudged the child, who had clearly been crying, and he handed me a small bi-lingual picture book which described the Kremlin.

'Dimitri didn't take this book,' I explained. 'We gave it to him. We have three small books we give to our young customers.'

Dimitri smiled. His shocked mother, who clearly didn't understand, thanked me. We had a policy that no child should leave the shop without a book. Financially this was possible because, prior to opening, I had purchased three hundred children's books, costing three cents apiece, from government-subsidized Russian bookstores.

Paying business taxes in Russia was quite different from paying them in the U.S.. After the Moscow papers had printed several articles about the problems of collecting what was owed, I asked one of our customers, who imported chicken to Russia, how he dealt with the issue.

He smiled and said, 'In Russia, the tax collectors come in person. Everything is negotiable.' Then he quickly looked down at our book table and asked. 'Is this place bugged?'

'Well, if it is, we didn't do it,' I replied.

He'd hit on a sore point. Some Russians thought we were a CIA front. At the same time, some Americans wondered if we were financed by the KGB. Later, when I asked Sasha if we paid business taxes, he also smiled.

'As much as anyone else,' he replied.

Yevgeny Yevtushenko, the Russian poet, whom we had met at the Soviet Writer's Union, invited Yuri and me to join him for drinks at a Moscow Hotel. As we prepared to drive off in his black Mercedes, he spotted a policeman stopping cars exiting the parking lot. Muttering something in Russian, he caused Yuri to laugh. As we approached the policeman, he shoved some rubles into his driver's license and breath mints in his mouth. 'I hope this guy likes poets,' he said. The cop shined his flashlight in our faces, pocketed the cash and waved us on.

Yevtushenko became my way to return favors that D. G. Wills and a La Jolla benefactor had done for me. Through the San

Diego Community Foundation, I had been awarded two grants for a California-Moscow network I organized to bring prominent Russians to San Diego State and the community. My benefactor and I had had lunch. On his suggestion I had written out a one-page letter describing the project and what I would do with requested funds; within two weeks thousands of dollars had arrived at the university, and a befuddled administrator was calling me,

'Mary, we have a check for your project, but we don't have any paperwork for it. Where is your grant request?'

'I didn't write one. I went to lunch.'

The university was happy with the money but not with my approach. Bureaucrats! The funds allowed me to bring Yevtushenko and other famous Russians to San Diego. He would read poetry to hundreds of students and customers at D. G. Wills. My benefactor – always invited to the events – said he enjoyed watching me spend his money.

Disaster struck in August 1998. The ruble collapsed and Russia's economy spiralled down. Dozens of American and other Western businesses closed; thousands of Westerners left Moscow. Our business slid like the rest of the economy; then, after about two months, it stabilized and we went back to making a profit, though never as high as before.

Slowly our customer base changed. Within a year seventy-five percent of our clients were Russian and only twenty-five Western, a reverse of before. We concentrated on selling inexpensive used books and paperbacks; but Sasha got tired of hosting the Saturday events, and they were suspended, even though customers petitioned him to continue. It was difficult for me to object, since I was only there about four months per year.

In 2000 Vladimir Putin was elected President. Under Yeltsin we had only had minor problems of officials shaking us down for bribes – twenty dollars here, fifty dollars there; nothing serious. After Putin's election the 'fines' escalated to a thousand, then fifteen hundred dollars.

Sasha had meanwhile turned much of his energy to his small publishing company, Ad Marginum, which specialized in avant-garde Russian writers. When Vladimir Sorokin wrote *Blue Fat*, a novel with a homosexual dream scene between Stalin and Khrushchev, Putin's people went crazy and raided the company, which shared facilities with the bookstore. They seized all the copies and fined Sorokin and Sasha $3000.

By 2002 Sasha had stopped paying me for the books I brought to Moscow. He blamed it on the fines. Unknown to me he had also stopped paying our other suppliers, and I arrived to find strangers working at Shakespeare and Co. When I confronted him, Sasha informed me that our written agreement had no 'juridical or legal merit': he had sold or rented the bookshop to a Russian woman without my permission. The store owed over $30,000 to creditors, he added. Shortly after, he bought himself a new apartment in downtown Moscow.

So it all ended – a story of doing business in the East in a 'Wild West' era. Still, I have to say that the eight years we spent building and operating Shakespeare and Co. in Moscow were some of the most memorable of my life. As Piaf sang, 'Je ne regrette rien.' The many satisfied customers, the new friends and joy of knowing that we had created a new literary tradition in Moscow more than compensated for the frustrations and disappointments with my partner.

People occasionally ask if I made a profit. Financially, if you factor in my airfares, I probably broke even.

In *The Moscow News* in 2005, Oleg Liakhovich wrote an article describing his personal experience at our shop:

'A few years ago I found a signed copy of Ferlinghetti's *A Coney Island of the Mind* in Shakespeare and Company. In the tradition of Sylvia Beach, Mary Duncan used to personally bring loads of books during her visits to Moscow, making it possible to find signed editions of Susan Sontag or the abovementioned Ferlinghetti. In the relaxed and stimulating atmosphere of the shop, it was not rare for a customer to spend an hour chatting with the owner about postmodernism and current tendencies in Russian literature, when all he wanted was to buy the latest John Grisham novel.'

This article captures the essence of what it felt like. I can add that it was always a thrill to hear a customer exclaim, 'Wow! I don't believe you have this book.'

The success of Shakespeare and Company, Moscow, became one of my great life satisfactions, a true labor of love. It seems summed up for me by the day an elderly woman walked in toting some used magazines. Overhearing the staff saying 'nyet' to her, I went over to see what was up.

'We told her these are too old for us to sell.'

Looking at what she had offered, I gasped. A large pile of *New Yorker*s from the 1950s were sitting on the desk. Quickly selecting one, I opened it. Words from Jean Genet's or Janet Flanner's 'Paris Journal' spread out before me.

'Where did they come from?'

Speaking in fluent English, the woman said that her late husband had been an English language translator and had worked for *The New Yorker*. (I never really quite understood how things like this happened under the Soviet regime.)

'How much do you want for them?'

'Two dollars.'

'Two dollars each is more than we can afford.'

'No. Two dollars for all.'

When I told her we would pay twenty-five cents apiece, she readily agreed and said she had many more from the '60s. Eagerly I bought all of them and resold them to appreciative customers. From then on every day when I had time I would sit in the lounge reading Genet or Flanner.

Paris had truly come to Moscow.

16. Pursuing Kafka's Last Love

With the experience of my bookstore, a transition had started in my life. At first I didn't recognize what was happening; then gradually I discovered I was forsaking political violence for more literary and cultural pursuits. This wasn't because the world had run out of bombed cities: Belfast had been replaced by strife in the Middle East, the Balkans, even New York. Looking back now, it's clear that I always veered towards this counterbalancing interest when in need of solace amidst the uncertainty of car bombs and gun-toting.

One organization more than any other kept me in touch with my literary enthusiasm, the Writing Women's group in San Diego. This group had started in 1988 in a writer's living-room as a support system for fifteen or so women working in a variety of areas from biography to cooking, children's stories, wild and domestic animals, newspaper features, memoirs and even my subject, the Irish Republican Army. After drinking wine and sharing dinner, we would each take a few minutes to discuss our latest project. We didn't critique each other's work, only asked questions and offered help if we could. It was here that I learned that the tortured genius, Franz Kafka, author of *The Trial*, *The Castle* and *Amerika* had had a lover about whom hardly anyone knew. And she had kept a diary.

Kathi Diamant, a member of our group, had been telling us for years about Dora Diamant, who tended to Kafka during the last eleven months of his life. Though sharing the same surname, Kathi didn't know if she and Dora were related; but thanks to her monthly updates, we knew a lot about the subject. Dora had met Kafka in Berlin, where he had been plagued by health problems. As his tuberculosis worsened, they had moved together to Vienna, where he died in 1924. Prior to his death, at his request, Dora had burned some of his papers and manuscripts, earning the eternal enmity of scholars. But like us, most people would never hear of Dora, until Kathi told them about her.

At a meeting in March 2000, Kathi mentioned that she had found one sentence in an old article by Marthe Robert, a French writer and translator of Kafka's work, which referred to Dora's *cahier* or diary. 'If I ever get to Paris,' she sighed, 'I'll try to find Dora's diary.'

'Kathi,' I said, 'I'm going to Paris this summer. If you like, I'll try to find the diary for you.'

Kathi knew the task would be difficult, even impossible; no one knew if the diary still existed, and Marthe Robert had died in 1996. Nevertheless, before I left for Paris, she brought me a bright red folder with a photograph of Kafka on front. Inside it were a two-page biography of him, a few paragraphs about Dora and a piece of paper containing two names: 'Colette Fans', identified as a longtime friend of Marthe Robert, and 'Michel Musan', Robert's husband. Handing me the folder, Kathi said, 'I hope they are still alive.' Also listed was Gallimard, Robert's French publisher.

Kathi knew that Dora could not have my undivided attention. The summer of 2000 was special for me: I was planning to buy my first Paris apartment. Even so, after a few days of seeing friends, getting over jet lag and looking at ads, I dropped by Gallimard and asked about Marthe Robert's papers and who might have information on them. The receptionist suggested I return in four days when the appropriate person would be back from vacation.

The following evening I was having dinner with Noel Riley Fitch and her husband Bert Sonnenfeld, whom I'd met after Noel's book *Sylvia Beach and the Lost Generation* was published. (At the time Noel and I had both been living in La Jolla.)

On this pleasant summer evening (actually, it was lousy weather, but Paris is always pleasant where I'm concerned) we were sitting in a restaurant on the Left Bank catching up with one another's lives when I mentioned that my literary task for the summer was to try to find Dora Diamant's diary. Noel and Bert were intrigued. They asked what I'd done so far.

'Not much, other than to visit Gallimard to ask about the deceased Marthe Robert.'

They both recognized the name.

'I'm trying to find two people,' I continued. 'One was a friend of Robert's and the other her husband. They must be quite elderly; Kathi doesn't know if they're still alive. If they are, we hope one of them will know something about the diary. The woman's name is Colette Fans.'

Bert looked startled. 'Do you mean Colette Faus?'

'No, Kathi wrote "Fans". I checked the phonebook, but she isn't listed.'

Bert and Noel glanced knowingly at each other. 'Mary,' Bert went on, 'Colette *Faus*, not Fans, was a very good friend of Marthe Robert. We're having dinner with her tomorrow night.' – They went on to explain that Colette's husband, Keeler Faus, had been a major source for Noel's book and that they knew him quite well. He had died a few years before, but they'd remained friends with Colette.

When excited, I don't sleep well. That dinner was the beginning of many sleepless nights.

I emailed Kathi and told her about the potential breakthrough. Two days later I called Colette.

My first rather undiplomatic response when she answered the phone was, 'Oh, my god! You're still alive.' Using Bert and Noel's names, I explained my mission and our wonder whether Marthe Robert's husband might have Dora Diamant's diaries. Colette corrected the spelling of his name to de M'uzan in capital letters. She said she was having lunch with him that Friday and gave me his phone number.

What luck! – I emailed Kathi again. Quickly she replied with questions to pose to de M'uzan, about photographs and letters. Then I called de M'uzan, who spoke some English. He asked me to write a letter detailing Kathi's questions. He would discuss it with Colette when he had lunch with her on Friday, he added; she could tell me about it when I next saw her, scheduled to be the next Monday afternoon.

From this chat with de M'uzan a surprise emerged. It turned out that Colette had been closer to Kathi than we realized. Having relatives in San Diego, she had been visiting on the same day that Kathi had given me the Kafka folder! – I emailed Kathi again and asked her to write a note to Colette describing what she'd done so far on the Dora biography. I also told her I was trying to borrow a tape recorder for the interview and complained about the rain, which was hindering my café lifestyle.

On the Sunday before our meeting, Colette phoned to say that de M'uzan had found some letters written in German between Dora and Marthe Robert. He had given them to her; she would show them to me at our meeting. She would also ask de M'uzan if she could make copies for Kathi. Adding a note of suspense, she mentioned that he had some other items but did not refer to a diary. In addition, in passing, she let drop that her deceased husband had been in charge of the American Embassy when the Germans had invaded France and after the liberation.

History was becoming part of my Kathi project.

This little intellectual adventure began pushing aside my other priorities, even the search for an apartment. A literary agent, whom Noel recommended, had started sending out book proposals for Kathi and had received some interest and some rejections but no real bites. The diary could make a difference.

'If I were in Belfast,' I asked myself, 'what would I do to maximize the impact of the interview with Colette?'

Armed with camera, tape recorder and notepad, plus all

the blarney my Irish ancestors had deposited in my genes, I arrived at a fine Art Deco building on the Boulevard Raspail at the time appointed. The neighborhood looked familiar. Simone de Beauvoir had lived a few blocks away, and Henry Miller had doubtless ridden his bicycle past when going from his apartment in Villa Seurat to meet friends at Le Select.

Colette opened the door. She was dressed in a blue print dress, and silver hair in a classic French cut framed her face. In her eighties, she was small – not much taller than me. Her English, which she'd learned in school, was impeccable.

While she prepared drinks – juice for me: I was not about to become inebriated – I eyed the papers on her coffee table. Courtesy dictated that I not rush straight into asking about the diaries, so once she had come back to settle on a brown leather sofa, I asked about the history of the building.

'Helena Rubenstein, the cosmetics magnate, had it designed and built for her family and her lover,' she said, raising a hand towards the high windows.

Colette went on to explain how she and her second husband, Keeler, had bought the apartment around 1950. Rubenstein, who died in 1965, had lived above. They always enjoyed listening to her and her sister laughing, playing cards and drinking late into the night. Regardless of this boisterousness, Helena had always been beautifully dressed the next morning when she'd gone to supervise her cosmetics empire.

Sartre had lived nearby, at 222 Boulevard Raspail. He and de Beauvoir had walked past together daily, on their trip from Café Flore to the Dome or one of their haunts in Montparnasse. Colette would see him buy his newspaper at a kiosk on the corner where Raspail met Montparnasse. Later, as his health had declined, she would see friends making the trip for him.

I asked Colette what life had been like during the German occupation. Her memories were still vivid sixty years on.

She was Catholic, but her first husband, Walter Allner – later art director for *Fortune* magazine – had been Jewish; and sometimes they had spent the night with friends so as not to be home if the Gestapo came calling. Whenever a car passed, the thought always was: are they coming to get us? 'It was a terrible way to live,' she mused. After they had a son, she helped Allner get to America. Later, they divorced.

During the war, she had worked in a food coupon distribution center. She had been able to steal coupons for friends. 'I fed at least eight people with those coupons, including a Romanian Jewish artist. One day he didn't come for his coupons, and I knew the Germans had finally picked him up... He gave me this bronze sculpture as a thank you.' Reaching into a tall, glass-lined bookshelf, she handed me a 12 inch high statue of a nude woman. 'So much tragedy, so much tragedy...'

We engaged in small talk, about Bert and Noel, the weather and her late husband. I was afraid to startle her with the recorder and camera, but as our attention turned to the papers I asked if I could tape our conversation for accuracy and so that Kathi could listen to it directly instead of having to rely on my account. By now, having heard her discuss World War II, I knew that Colette was not easily intimidated. She said yes.

Moments later I was holding Dora's original *cahier*, looking at photographs and sorting through letters. With the recorder on, I carefully counted out forty handwritten pages of *cahier*, as well as eighty pages of a 'Journal de Dora' plus fifteen letters Dora had written to Marthe Robert. There were also three pages of Dora's notes, one written in Yiddish, and ten letters from another friend to Robert.

My immediate impulse was to grab all this stuff and run, but of course I didn't. As a consolation, I had Colette photograph me holding the *cahier*.

Graciously, she continued to answer questions, adding details to enhance interest of the materials. Marthe Robert had died of TB. She had smoked four packs a day and had only lived as long as she had because Michel de M'uzan was a doctor. They had never divorced and lived together until she died, even though he had another woman, whom Colette didn't name. Colette and Marthe had met as children and were lifelong friends.

Confirming that she visited San Diego twice a year, Colette said she would like to meet Kathi. Then came the bad news/good news. The bad was that she would have to convince de M'uzan to let her make copies of the materials, and nothing could be guaranteed. She would have lunch with him again on the Friday; I was to call her again the following Monday. The good news was that no one else has seen the *cahier*, journal or letters.

I emailed Kathi that, although we didn't have the materials, I was hopeful. Due to the nine-hour time difference, she was now practically sleeping next to her computer.

She zipped back an excited reply: 'Mary, I'm beyond words, other than to say, I HAVE to have copies of those things!... Is there anything I can do?... send her flowers?'

'Flowers aren't necessary. I took her some caviar. She knows she has us by the balls (pardon my language). She may dangle the materials, but I think you'll get them.' – I added the suggestion that Kathi write letters thanking both Colette and de M'uzan for their cooperation and meeting with me. But, I said, 'Don't be too fawning.'

Kathi copied our emails to her literary agent and described the discovery of the cache of materials. The agent sent these on to publishers who had expressed an interest but not yet offered a contract. Two publishers responded; and on July 14, Bastille Day in France, Kathi was able to report that one of them had made an offer on the book. 'It's a little low, so we haven't accepted it yet, but it's an offer! You're the new hero of the Writing Women. I've spoken to Tershia [another member] who says I must hold a parade in your honor.'

'Well, I'm only half a hero. We know what exists and where it is, but we don't have a positive answer. I'm to call Colette on Monday... Spent Bastille Day with champagne, caviar, and dessert at a friend's apt overlooking the Eiffel Tower, watching fireworks. I love this city!'

As promised, I called Colette Monday morning.

The news was not good. De M'uzan hadn't made up his mind and wouldn't know before September, when he returned from holiday. Colette still had the materials and said she might copy them. She had emphasized to de M'uzan that Kathi had Dora's family's support and felt he would agree but stressed that he didn't make rapid decisions.

Kathi and I were both frustrated. We were so close, yet couldn't get a positive commitment.

Kathi sent Colette a *vita*, along with a new list of what she'd accomplished with the Dora project. I took Colette to lunch and tried to be nice without being obvious. In spite of not having better news for Kathi, I remained optimistic.

Kathi then sent a lengthy email that raised another issue. 'When I told Dora's family and my advisory committee the good news of your discovery, a Kafka scholar wrote back furious that he's not the one who gets to find it. I just don't want him complicating anything now that I've failed (temporarily) to get the copies… I should have known that it wouldn't be simple or easy or inexpensive.'

I assured Kathi that Colette had done all she could, and I offered to help with and pay for the copying, but her desperation was now showing:

'If I come to Paris,' the next email said, 'will Colette let me see the papers? I wouldn't mind being disappointed about the copies if I could see the originals. I can read German, and at least I'd know if there are any bombshells… Waaaaaaah! I want to see the originals!'

Feeling the need for advice, I emailed Noel, whom I'd kept informed about the meeting with Colette. Noel advised that we shouldn't pressure Colette and stressed the importance of building a relationship. If we pushed it, we could ruin our opportunity. Noel was also concerned about other scholars 'mucking about', now that they knew who had the diaries. She didn't think Colette was playing games, but clearly she realized how valuable the materials were and didn't want to be hasty.

Fear of other scholars interfering or trying to hijack the diaries was legitimate. Biographers actively protect sources, particularly where new materials are concerned. The literary world is rife with intrigue, betrayal and theft when researchers are competing for the same information. Knowing this, I tried to guide Kathi.

'When I call Colette on Monday,' I said in my next email, 'I think I shouldn't even mention the papers and let you do that via mail. I'll talk about her deceased husband and her visit to San Diego. She's clearly a little lonely in SD, because her hosts work during the day – she's invited me to swim at their home. Noel stressed the importance of building a relationship. I don't know what else to say.'

In the middle of this drama, I was finally getting around to doing what I'd come to Paris to do: find an apartment and live in French style. A friend had recommended a hair salon, and I was showing off a new haircut. Meanwhile, Kathi wrote back thanking me for my advice. Everything was on hold now until September, when de M'uzan returned from his vacation.

Three days later, Kathi sent another email. It had the best news: 'Mary and Noel! Dora's biography has a U.S. publisher – The Free Press: a division of Simon and Schuster. I'm very excited. I can point to the two of you as being directly behind this? Thanks for all your help, encouragement and support!'

I responded, congratulating her, then told her *my* news. I'd found an apartment, and my offer had been accepted! In approximately ninety days a small studio in the 7th arrondissement, between Duroc and Vaneau metro stations, would be mine. Even though it was only 25 meters or 250 square feet – probably smaller than my double garage in La Jolla – I was jubilant. Located in a traditional 18th century building, it had high ceilings, hardwood floors and a marble fireplace. It needed work, but nothing compared to what I'd done on mountain cabins in Idyllwild twenty years before. I was paying cash so I didn't have to worry about a mortgage.

These excitements were followed by more good news. Colette called to say I could have copies of Dora's diaries, though Kathi couldn't have permission to use them until de M'uzan gave it.

I wrote Kathi that I was on an emotional roller-coaster and she could buy the Margaritas at José's the next time I was in La Jolla. 'Mary,' she wrote back, 'I'm literally holding my breath. Two more days! I know what you mean by roller-coaster. The book deal and this have got me going up and down and inside out. Make that Margaritas and dinner, too.'

Two days later, bad news. After looking at more photos of Colette's husband and grandchildren and listening to more war stories, I left empty-handed. Colette said that, when de M'uzan returned, she would talk to him about copies; that was all. There was no point in me protesting. I had to content myself with her showing me the letter she had received from Kathi and saying she was looking forward to meeting her.

I wrote Kathi and said we were now at Colette's mercy. I added hopefully that at least we did know the materials existed and where they were. As regards others contacting de M'uzan, at least they couldn't do it before September.

We were torn between exhilaration and emotional exhaustion. To know where the diaries were but still not have access was almost Kafkaesque itself. After all our efforts, there was the disastrous possibility that Colette or de M'uzan would not consent to Kathi seeing or using the diaries.

Feeling that I had done all I could, I turned the task of continuing the pursuit over to Kathi and returned to San Diego. She went on corresponding with Colette and de M'uzan, restating her purpose and asking once again to see the materials. Finally, without knowing whether she would ever receive copies, she flew to Paris on October 9th.

'I went to Paris specifically to get the diaries,' she would write to me. 'I had to try. I did have to wait a couple of days for Colette to receive me, but when she did, she already had the copies. She had made them all herself – a huge job! I also met with M'U during that visit, too, and was able to hold and look through the originals.'

She flew back to San Diego on October 17th with the copies in her luggage. Her book *Kafka's Last Love* (Basic Books, 2003) revealed that, while Dora had kept silent about Kafka for most of her life after his death, in later years she'd wanted to set the record straight and correct the myriad misunderstandings that had cropped up about who he had been and what he had intended. Dora had expressed frustration at her lack of ability to write in any language well enough to say what she wanted to say about Kafka. Most of her diaries and letters were in German, but Yiddish was her first language.

Kathi learned that it was Dora who had encouraged the first French translations of Kafka's work. She had offered to use her own money from the royalties she'd received to finance the publishing of his diaries. Dora had also visited Paris in February 1950 to meet Jean-Louis Barrault, the French actor/director, who produced a film version of *The Trial*.

The story doesn't end there. *Kafka's Last Love* explains how Dora had destroyed Kafka's work at his insistence, not out of her wish. At the time, she had been only 24 years old and did as he ordered, burning them in front of his eyes. She didn't burn everything, however. In 1933, when Hitler came to power, the Gestapo had raided Dora's Berlin apartment and confiscated all the remaining materials related to Kafka. No one knew if these still existed. Kathi decided to try to locate them.

In 1996, as part of her Kafka Project at San Diego State, Kathi had filed a petition with the German government to search for the seized writings. In 1998 documentation had been found proving the confiscation, but none of the letters and papers could be found, and the search continues. There were, however, some rewarding discoveries. German archives revealed that Dora had relations in Israel who didn't know that she, or each other, existed. That and other information led to a joyous family reunification in Tel Aviv. They only lived ten minutes apart from one another.

Two years prior to retrieving the diaries, Kathi had felt there was something she had to do. When Dora had died of nephritis in 1952, she had been buried in an unmarked grave in the United Synagogue Cemetery in East Ham, London. Her daughter, Marianne, who died in 1982, had been interred elsewhere. Kathi, along with Dora's family, friends and Kafka scholars, organized a stone-setting for Dora. Thus on August 15, 1999, forty-seven years after Dora's death, a graveside service had been held for Dora and Marianne.

Kathi ended her book with a description of it:

'Marianne's name was included on Dora's beautiful white marble headstone, which is engraved with both their names, along with a quotation by Robert Klopstock', who had helped care for Kafka. On the day after Kafka died, Klopstock had written: 'Who knows Dora, knows what love means.'

17. Back to Belfast

My husband Yuri's most dreaded words from me were not 'Please do the dishes, dear' but 'I'm bored'. He knew from experience that these two words could provoke a creative venture like the Moscow store, or buying books I would never read, or purchasing a painting I would hate later. But in the summer of 2004, in spite of thriving Paris cafés, discovery of Dora's diary, travel to Italy, helping out with a literary festival and dinners with friends, a familiar angst began to settle over me. I felt the need for some serious stimulation with a touch of past danger.

Due to the news of peace talks, much lower incidences of violence and reports of an increase in tourism, Belfast was on my mind. Although I had made numerous trips there in the previous thirty years, now was the time to find the answers to questions remaining. I also wanted to do something I had never been able to afford in the old days. To stay at the Europa Hotel, recently overtaken by the Holiday Inn in Sarajevo as the 'most bombed hotel in the world'.

The Europa, once known as 'Hotel Erupta', had become the elegant four-star Hastings Europa. Instead of shattered, boarded up windows, it had a doorman, plush carpeting, marble floors and comfortable sofas in the lobby. For the first time, I signed the register and was conducted to a ninth floor suite overlooking the Falls Road, once the Provisional Irish Republican Army stronghold, where many battles had begun and ended.

I was soon visited by a friend I'd known for years. Johnny had served time for terrorist activities, but now he was wearing a pressed shirt and tailored slacks instead of scruffy blue jeans and a worn t-shirt.

He gave me a friendly hug, looking around the room, shrugged and said, 'I doubt that it's bugged anymore. What's on your mind, Duncan?'

The Belfast guys had always called me by my last name, even when introducing me to others.

Now that the Provos had declared a ceasefire and almost all troubles-related prisoners had been released, I could feel safe in asking him, 'I'm curious. About the bombings here, where we're standing – what procedures did the Provos use when they called in the bomb warnings?'

'Ah,' he grinned, 'that I can answer. Purely from a hearsay stance, you understand.' – Taking a sip of the coffee provided by room service, he explained, 'They had code words but they rarely called the police directly. The Samaritans were usually the go-between.'

The Samaritans were a twenty-four hour community hotline. They had relayed the messages to the security forces, who would then call the Europa.

'What code words did the Provos use?'

He told me the history of one code word: 'Eagle'. From a payphone, the Provo would say, 'This is Eagle calling. There's a bomb at the Europa. You have thirty minutes.' 'Eagle' was used during the 1970s to confirm that a bomb had been planted at a prestige target or an R.P.G.7 (a Soviet-made rocket-propelled grenade, then a favorite of the IRA) had struck a British armored vehicle. The Provos combined a sense of humor with history in selecting the word. When the Apollo 11 moon flight had arrived on the moon on July 20, 1969, the astronauts had announced, 'The Eagle has landed.'

'Is it true Johnny, that in the early days, a lot of the guys blew themselves up while learning to make bombs?'

'Mary, are you planning to become a wee bomber in America?

'No, but I am curious.'

Waving a finger at me, he said, 'You know what they say about cats?'

Initially, they had used car batteries, alarm clocks, even wooden dowels the size of a pencil sitting in a hole on top of a box separating the detonator and timer. When the rod was pulled, the timer would start to tick. Later bombs had more sophisticated delayed-action timers. An engineer from a local telephone company designed many of the early bombs, Johnny said, using expertise he had learned on the job. When he'd complete a bomb, he'd give it to a member of a front-line active service unit of the Provos, who would deliver it to the Europa. 'He disappeared,' Johnny sighed, 'when he became a liability' – meaning, I assume, that the Provos had killed him.

Johnny admitted that the security forces and the British Army bomb disposal squads hadn't been stupid. As they'd become more adept at disarming devices, the Provos had developed even more dangerous anti-handling bombs, designed to explode at the slightest touch. The Europa had meanwhile established a bomb-warning system of ringing bells, staff alerts and evacuation procedures. A notice in every room warned the visitor that, 'because of the civil unrest in Belfast, you may have to speedily evacuate the building'.

After a Europa Hotel bombing Provo supporters would, as I've said, gather at the Felons Club to celebrate another successful blow to British prestige. I asked Johnny about the current status of the club. He laughed and said he hadn't been back there for years and, if I wanted to know how the Felons had deterred and frustrated the security forces' raids, I'd have to go and ask them myself. We parted, he agreeing to come back to meet me again before I checked out.

I walked by modern, newly constructed buildings to a taxi rank. I reflected on Paris and how it had helped me survive and even thrive in Belfast and other potentially dangerous places. Paris had enabled me to cope better with the ugly surrealism of much of our world. In the 1980s, after leaving Belfast or other strife-ridden spots, I had always yearned for Paris. Even after I was no longer going to Belfast or the like on a regular basis, Paris was what I longed for – to heal a broken heart, to escape disappointments at the university or family problems, to find a moment of sanity or to celebrate new accomplishments, such as the opening of a Moscow bookstore.

I observed the contrasts between the Belfast of now and of my earlier years. As a black taxi drove me by a familiar mural of Bobby Sands, the hunger striker, who'd died in '81, we passed Milltown Cemetery where many Provos, as well as some of their victims, are buried. Then the large, green, two-story Felons Club came into view. The driver dropped me off.

The Irish Republican Felons Association – its official name – stood like a mini-fortress on Andersonstown Road in West Belfast. Andytown, as called by locals, was a Catholic stronghold with a bloody history; the club had been here since 1973. One block away the Northern Ireland authorities had recently bulldozed and demolished Andersonstown Barracks, with its hated barbed wire and steel sides, which had housed the security forces. No one missed the irony of which building had survived more than thirty years of 'the troubles'.

Many years earlier, because of the broad Belfast accent, I had thought the Felons was named Fallon's Club after a character in *Dynasty*, the American television show. The laugh was on me. I hadn't known that most of its members were convicted felons who had served time for political or, depending on whom you asked, terrorist-related offenses. The club was basically a social refuge for the Provos and their pals.

When I got up to the heavy iron gates, a rough, male voice greeted me, asking what I wanted. 'I'm writing about the changes in Belfast and would like to visit the club,' I replied. A buzzer sounded; I smiled for the security camera and opened the gate. To the left was a man monitoring a sophisticated array of nine small video screens. He could see the entrance, gate, exits, storeroom, main bar rooms and across the street.

Visiting the Felon's four times in my three days, I was able to unfold its history. Approximately five hundred members and associates paid about eight dollars a year to belong. Nelson Mandela and Brian Keenan, a former hostage in Lebanon, were honorary members. The late John F. Kennedy, Jr., when he was publishing *George* magazine, had interviewed Gerry Adams, the president of Sinn Fein, political arm of the IRA, while drinking beer here.

After much coaxing, Danny Morrison, a Board member, who had been interned and served four and a half years, explained that three main tactics were used to thwart raids of the security services. First they would be delayed at the main gate as long as possible, perhaps a couple of minutes. Second, men who were wanted would hide or slide out the back door – it was in fact considered a badge of courage for a wanted man to appear at the Felons, knowing he risked arrest if the club was raided.

The third tactic, according to Morrison, was to harass the troops once they'd entered the club. The men would turn their faces to the wall, making it difficult for any that were wanted to be identified. Sometimes members would start singing Provo songs such as 'My Little Armalite'. Most disruptive was when men and women would bang their bottles on the bar and tables while shouting obscenities at the forces. This usually ended with several men being arrested. Often, however, there was only absolute quiet, with the customers glaring at the intruders.

Those days were gone now. Liam Shannon, another Felons Board member, said that several years had passed since the last raid, and then it had only been to seize bar receipts to see if liquor was being served after closing time.

Some habits die hard. A few men were sitting by an exit or a window with their backs to the wall, facing the entrance. This classic get-away position for men on the run wasn't really necessary, since hardly anyone was wanted now. When I asked if I could take a couple of photos, a member standing nearby loudly said, 'The lady is taking photos', and everyone at the bar turned their backs on me.

The Felons is now open to the public. The Provos declared a ceasefire on August 11, 2005. The Club has a small museum with artefacts from Long Kesh, the prison where most members had done their 'wack', or time. It's a reminder of why the club came to exist. The collection includes a wooden hand-carved rocking chair, Irish harps, plaques commemorating dead members and some jewellery.

In my jewellery box in La Jolla is a small metal ring, designed with an Irish harp on it. It was given to me years ago by a former prisoner. That ring would have been an instant conversation piece and meant easier access to the inner sanctum of the Felons in the old days.

I'll wear it on my next visit to Belfast, I thought.

Outside the Felons, I walked for a while, then flagged down another black cab. Peace had indeed come to Belfast. I didn't see any British soldiers on the Falls Road, military vehicles or anti-British graffiti.

On my last afternoon at the Hastings Europa, I met Johnny again and asked him why peace had arrived.

'Several things happened. Money dried up from Libya and other sources. Demographically, the Catholic population is catching up with the British Protestant population, and Sinn Fein is winning more seats in Parliament.'

Part of Sinn Fein's success is due to the constituency services it provides for Catholic residents, which it learned in Boston and New York from Democratic Party precinct workers. Johnny also said that British intelligence had infiltrated Provos and that the economy had improved.

'You know,' he then observed, 'you Irish Americans did donate to the Provos, but you were far from its biggest financial supporters. The British taxpayers funded them through its social services. Most armies have to provide housing, food, health care and uniforms for their members; most Provos members and their families were on the dole [welfare], which often continued even if a family member was jailed for terrorist activities. Provos channelled the money into arms, transportation and printing presses.'

We turned our attention to the panoramic view over the now-quiet city. Again looking out over the Falls Road, he said,

'Who'd have ever thought thirty years ago, that you'd be living in Paris and we'd be enjoying room service in a suite at the Hastings Europa Hotel?'

Very true. But Johnny didn't know the secret that had brought me so often to Northern Ireland. When a reporter had once asked me if I wasn't afraid of getting hurt or killed in Belfast, I'd replied,

'I'm more afraid of dying bored than of dying.'

18. Henry Miller is Under My Bed

While cleaning out my university office, sorting through lecture notes and old Belfast files, I saw two audio-taped interviews with Bradley Smith clatter to the floor. Inserting one into a recorder, I heard Bradley again discussing with his old friend their mutual prostate problems. While he and Henry commiserated about potential effects on their sex lives, my mind flashed back to manuscripts, tapes and photographs from *My Life and Times* and *Insomnia*. What had happened to them? Had Mara Vivat ever sold them? Who held the rights? I began wondering... Would she sell them to me?

In December 2005 I'd retired from San Diego State. My finances had improved, which meant there was time and money for intellectual pursuits other than what was required by academe. Perhaps I should become a cultural entrepreneur, I thought. Henry might be a good place to start.

After Bradley's death in 1997, his companion Mara had become his literary executor. When she'd moved out of his house, she'd asked me if I would store the Miller materials in a safe place. 'Sure,' I'd replied; and for the next two years Henry had rested in sealed, flat boxes under my bed, waiting to be retrieved and shared with the world.

Books, photographs, correspondence, manuscripts and transcripts of interviews he'd done with Bradley – Henry had teased me with his presence just a few inches below my mattress. Many of the items were originals with comments in his own hand. Occasionally, I'd pull out a box and look through the large black and white photographs of him and his family or read parts of manuscripts, moving my fingers over his writing. The sound of his voice answering Bradley's questions about Paris, love, sex, philosophy, art, writing, life and death flowed through my psyche. I'd always coveted these materials, I realized. Now they lay under my bed, wanting, I thought, to be mine.

Eventually, Mara moved to larger living quarters and reclaimed Henry. Later she asked me to help sell him to a university library. We made contact with the Ransom Research Center at the University of Texas at Austin, which already had some Miller stuff. She negotiated for months, but I didn't know if a transaction had been completed.

Bradley's voice on the tapes pulled me back. A tingle shot up my spine. Old feelings of being on the hunt surged as I contemplated the possibility that the tapes had never been sold. Could Mara still have them? In my rush to drive home from my office and call her, I probably threw out files I should have kept. After a phone call to Elizabeth, Bradley's fifth wife, now widow (I was amazed at how people linked to Bradley, even former wives, stayed in touch), I had Mara's new phone number in Kauai, Hawaii, where she had moved with John Aster, her companion. Taking a deep breath and crossing my fingers, I called. We chatted and caught up on one another's lives. Then came the big question: had she sold Henry?

'No,' she replied. 'He's here in the garage. I still have him.'

My breath quickened. 'Mara,' I said finally, 'I'm interested in buying him, as a retirement present for myself. It would be a great project for Paris.'

Enthusiastically, she agreed. We actually settled on a price. She promised to mail me the tapes the next day.

Not long after, while browsing an antiquarian bookstore in La Jolla and impatiently waiting for Henry to arrive, I met Yousef Khanfar, a writer and photographer. Yousef had overheard me asking the owner if he had any books by or about Miller. As the owner went off to search his shelves, Yousef inquired why I should be interested in Henry Miller.

Good question. I'm not a Miller scholar or literature professor; through Bradley, however, I had developed a very personal connection to Henry. Paris was part of it. More than that, Henry's survival instincts drew me, also his romanticism in walking away from a job he'd hated, going abroad, living by his wits, borrowing money from friends and writing 'dirty' books. Telling Yousef about my impending purchase, I said, 'This is an impulse buy, a labor of love – I've wanted them for years.' He suggested organizing the materials into a travelling exhibit to cross the United States. Even Europe might be possible.

All of a sudden Henry had become an upward learning curve for me. Each day brought something new, as I savored possible projects the acquisition might bring. Then too, like Henry, I was trying to walk away from a job that no longer brought the satisfaction it once had.

My last ten years at SDSU had not been particularly happy. Tired of the departmental politics and backstabbing, I'd memorized the Calpers (California Public Employees' Retirement System) chart, showing what your retirement income might be after combining the number of years you had worked, your age and your highest annual salary. I was dismayed with the way the administration had mishandled an innovative on-line learning program which a colleague had created. The university could have had the leading program in the country; instead, because of the bureaucrats' inept reaction to something they did not understand, it was left with amateurish cyberspace technology. Impatient for a time when I could afford to dump this second-rateness completely, I'd grown acutely aware that I was hooked on the 'golden handcuffs' I had warned students about. The salary, health benefits, flexible hours and pleasant working conditions I'd taken advantage of by signing up to an early retirement program had permitted me to teach one semester a year. Four months of work had enabled me to be 'retired' for eight, which is how – reaching for the gold ring – I'd been able to move to Paris for much of the year.

It's true that I had flourished at my university, and I was grateful to it for the chance to become the blend of teacher and scholar it encouraged. Tales from my research adventures had spilled over into my classes, from the rubber and plastic bullets of Belfast to a Russian husband and life in Moscow. In courses focused on work, leisure, consumerism and happiness, I had joked that I practiced the leisure. I wouldn't just tell students that money can't buy happiness, but I would quote research showing that the number of friends you had would contribute more to it than the material things you could buy. At the same time, I cautioned against elite bigotry – a form of discrimination Max Lerner had warned me about long before.

Elite bigotry Max had defined as discrimination against people who had fewer degrees or a less prestigious education than you. It could be as damaging as sex discrimination, religious discrimination, racism or class discrimination, he had contended. Elite bigotry was typified by the person who in the first five minutes of conversation would casually drop a word about his Ivy League alma mater or graduate degrees. Max, who was sensitive about his degree from Yale, had felt you must never undervalue a person's life experiences.

The research and travel that dominated my career while teaching had been salvation from the alienation I'd felt inside academic walls. My ability to create a parallel life partly separate from my department, of which much of this book is about, had helped keep angst at bay. Henry Miller had helped too. He had demonstrated that survivors make different choices, that frequently they have standards and ethics different from those of people raised in more middle-class environments, that they bend rules, seek alternative solutions to problems, use different criteria for measuring success or failure and learn to think outside the norms society dictates.

I longed to have Henry again under my bed.

When the tapes arrived on Christmas Eve, I carefully unwrapped them. Each still had Bradley's handwritten description, with dates and content. What an incredible present! I placed one tape in the recorder. The strong, solid voice with Brooklyn accent filled the room.

In the course of one passage, Henry described how he had caught clap at a whorehouse in National City, California. *What?* I stopped the tape, played it back. A whorehouse in National City? My hometown! This revelation made me think that my impulsive purchase had been providential.

National City had always been a poor stepsister to San Diego. Though it had worked hard in recent years to change its image with a marina and redevelopment program, it was still considered 'the wrong side of the tracks'. As a nineteen year old in 1910 Henry had worked on a ranch in nearby Otay – even closer to the Mexican border – clearing brush. On the tape he described a poster he had seen in National City advertising a speech that Emma Goldman, the anarchist, was going to give in San Diego. That lecture, he said, changed his life. Goldman's views on free love or sex without societal restraint, along with the anarchist's creed of questioning all authority, had appealed to his rebel spirit.

On another tape, while discussing his writing, Henry let drop that in National City he had experienced for the first time a complete loss of identity. How strange I thought: he lost his sense of identity in the very town where mine was forged. Paris, on the other hand, is where he said he'd found freedom. Likewise, I thought.

Everyday I listened to these tapes as I waited for the photos, manuscripts and correspondence to arrive. They didn't, and I became increasingly frustrated.

In January 2006, I flew back to Paris with copies of the tapes but not the other materials. March came and, despite several emails and phone calls, no Henry.

To be so close and yet so far from having him was beginning to feel as though I had a lover with whom there was a lot of foreplay but no climax – a situation of which Henry himself would have vehemently disapproved. No money had exchanged hands. At this point there was only a simple verbal agreement between Mara and me.

April arrived. Mara sent copies of publishing contracts between Bradley and Henry; still, no photos or other important materials. I set off on my semi-annual trip to New York to visit my godsons, five year old Max and two year old Luca. As the family sat in its apartment hearing my story about Henry, something struck me – New York City is already half way to Hawaii!

Of course! If I wanted the materials, I needed to go get them. A quick email to John and Mara... They invited to me visit now, instead of the following January, as previously planned. I threw away my return ticket to Paris and flew to Kauai.

Kauai has a similar ruggedness to Big Sur where Henry lived from 1942 to 1960. The sun, the beaches, the beautiful women, the tranquillity and isolation away from big cities all would have inspired him, I'm sure.

Sitting in the living-room of Mara and John, two blocks from a beach overlooking the blue sea, we compared stories about Bradley and laughed. His memories of Henry were meanwhile packed in two large filing cabinets, several photograph folders and boxes. No wonder Mara hadn't known what to send me.

As soon as I was shown to the materials, I started to sort through them. Mara brought a large box of photos up to the dining-room table; every few minutes something would catch my eye and I stop to look or to read. Contracts with *Playboy*, letters, notes with Henry's signature scrawled at the bottom, thousands of negatives and original photos used in the production of *My Life and Times* and *Insomnia*... Progress was slow. It was four days before the photocopying of a large pile began. Two days after that, I flew back to Paris with two new, large blue suitcases filled with Henry.

Reading all the materials, looking at the photographs again and listening to the tapes made it even more clear to me why I had been so intuitively attracted. Henry gave us permission to live free from the unjustified, permission to say 'fuck it'. As Erica Jong wrote, he had 'the courage to be an individual, no matter what the consequences.' Like Henry, I believed in living life as an individual, taking my knocks and having a hell of a time doing it. On the opening page of *Tropic of Cancer*, he had written, 'I have no money, no resources, no hopes. I am the happiest man alive.'

We can all learn from this.

Epilogue: Chez Moi

When a publisher expressed interest in my attempting to write a memoir, I realized that I could no longer put off what I am doing now. Henry helped propel me into action.

I found myself scribbling most mornings from nine to one. Sometimes the process would begin at five. Whenever it grew tedious or I became blocked, I would listen to Henry talk about his philosophy of life or struggles as a writer. He had written best twenty years after the event, the voice said, which was mostly what I was doing. He would compile a lot of notes that he would rarely use when setting down words. But by that magical process that writing gradually teaches, putting down his thoughts helped him compress them until they came out 'like water from a faucet'.

My attempts have not evolved in exactly the same way. Still, I've felt Henry's presence while musing at my dining-room table in this small Paris apartment; and his books and tapes have sometimes crept out from under my bed as I've typed and I hear his voice saying, 'I'm writing, that's the important thing.'

Sometimes too I work sitting upstairs in the 'Non Fumeur' area of Café de la Mairie, one of his favorite spots. There from the booth I like best I occasionally look down to the street and see an old pigeon lady feeding her feathered friends and casually brushing their poop off of the shoulders of her baggy coat. Did he see the same woman strolling there when she was pretty and young?

Expatriate friends often ask each other how they came to live in Paris. Each has a story, some familiar, some funny, some a quirk of fate. Henry came to Paris by accident: his original destination had been Spain.

The compass for my journey may have been designed by a con-artist. In San Diego when I was in my twenties, Charles Simmons, a dynamic motivational speaker, used to give seminars on how you could change your life. As part of a six-month course, he would ask students to complete financial forms outlining their assets; he would then use the information to lure them into 'investment' schemes. Imprisoned for fraud, he died of a heart attack while driving on a Texas road in the 1970s.

I didn't lose any money to Simmons, because I didn't have any to lose. But I absorbed his rules for achieving goals in life.

The rules he taught were modified from the book *Think and Grow Rich* by Napoleon Hill (1937). The ironic coincidence of Hill's first name used to amuse me: Napoleon was a planner who ended disastrously, but he still dominates French history. Hill had adapted his rules from Andrew Carnegie, the great industrialist/philanthropist. Simmons had distilled them further into nine distinctive steps.

'Desire is the first step to achieving a goal or dream,' he would shout from the stage. 'A fire in your belly – you have to feel it *here,*' pointing to his small protruding paunch.

Simmons urged us to let an all-consuming objective dominate our thoughts. In class lectures, when I would give my students his version of 'How to Get What You Want Out of Life', I would mention Bill Gates, Nelson Mandela, Oprah Winfrey, Lenin, Martin Luther King, Mother Teresa and Hitler as examples. Some of their dreams benefited the world, others almost destroyed it. Simmons, by contrast, made each of us feel that we could fulfil our dreams while not hurting anyone.

With his silver hair and moustache highlighted against a dark blue suit, he would pace back and forth, stressing the importance of deadlines. '*Sometime* never comes,' he would admonish. Time lines had to be specific and measurable – not necessarily a specific day, but a time frame such as 'by the end of Summer, 2009'.

Simmons would ask his seminar suckers to write down what they wanted. 'Go into action. Put it on paper. Make a commitment to yourself,' he would yell, waving a piece of paper in air. That simple action would reinforce the desire. If living in Paris was your goal, then other easy tasks such as phoning a travel agency, buying a French language cassette or reading related books would create a link between it and the achievement.

Carnegie had said, 'Like minds attract one another.' Simmons changed this to the simple axiom, 'Go to the experts' – in other words, discuss your plan with people who can help or encourage you. Seek out those who have accomplished what you are trying and get them involved in helping you achieve your dream. Simmons insisted that people liked to help one another.

He knew our weak points. Sarcastically, he would warn, 'Don't blab your dreams to everyone you know. Be a doer, not a talker.' For me, this was one of his most difficult rules: when excited or challenged, I was prone to tell the world. But Simmons was right: blabbing creates energy leaks. Focus that energy; don't dissipate it. Once the experts have been consulted, their advice can be used to formulate a long-range plan. Don't let the size of the mountain discourage you; break it down into manageable pieces.

Manageable pieces for me would mean short forays to Paris – a week here, a month there. On each visit I made a new friend, dined in a different restaurant, walked around a different neighborhood. I started building a foundation.

Money, ah money. Paris is expensive. How to afford this dream? – Simmons would stress that finances could not be ignored. (It was part of his way to lure you into his get rich schemes.) Paris is filled with numerous Americans and other expatriates who come with a dream and get their hearts broken. Living like Henry Miller lived is nearly impossible now. Visa restrictions, work permits and high rents conspire to thwart future Hemingways, Josephine Bakers, James Joyces. Financial planning is essential.

Financial planning, I learned, meant putting myself first – not all the time, but certainly part of it. I had watched parents, female in particular, putting themselves last – a daughter's wedding, college expenses, braces for kids' teeth, a husband's dream-car ate up what had been saved for their own dream. I set aside a nest egg even when it was only a few dollars a time.

'Be careful of what you wish for. You may get it.' While Simmons had emphasized the importance of focusing on a goal, he'd warned against myopic thinking. Alternatives provide flexibility. Was Paris really for me? – I tried living in Russia. For a time it had consumed my energy as Shakespeare and Co. Moscow had blossomed. Paris, however, kept drawing me back. It nourished my soul.

Pointing at us from the stage, Simmons would cry, 'There is no free lunch! You have to pay your dues. Everything worthwhile has a price.' Then a couple of his previous students would stand up so he could tell us about the obstacles they'd overcome and successes they'd achieved after completing his course. Most involved acquiring more money or material assets.

I knew the next step well: assessing the liabilities of accomplishing my goal – the early morning phonecall telling me my nephew Troy had died without me being able to see him again; the email to say that Alice di Gesu, my ninety-four year old friend, had succumbed from a routine hospital procedure and I couldn't get home in time for her memorial service. On the lighter note, think of all the Monday night Margaritas with Joanie I would miss at José's!

Simmons, a clever charlatan, had kept students focused on their dreams while fleecing their pockets. Greed was easy to manipulate, because most wanted to get rich. One woman, however, had only wanted to walk again. Injured in a tragic car accident, her brain had been damaged; her talking was difficult, and she was paralyzed and in a wheelchair. On the last night of the course, we each were required to speak about how we were achieving our dream. With the help of her husband, she had simply stood up and walked several steps.

It taught a lesson for the ones with the material dreams, like buying an apartment building or a new Mercedes. It underlined that existence of the simple faculties of life was more important. Good health, love, relationships, trust, persistence and loyalty trump the dollar bill.

My dream had been to meet interesting people and see the world – rather vague and idealistic for a girl from National City still grateful for the public parks, tennis facilities and library that gave a refuge and foundation on which to build. Wrapping myself up in Simmons chain, I discovered its weak links, broke it and announced that I was going to join the Peace Corps – which I did. The Peace Corps, however, like the Girl Scouts and my sorority, had a hierarchical structure; and conformity, as I think I've shown on these pages, was not my strong suit. Rebelling against the peer evaluation forms and simulation games that I felt divided rather than unified our group, I tried to organize the other volunteers to sit these out. My attempt failed, and I was sent back to San Diego crying and broken-hearted. I didn't get to Malaysia, but I did see De Kalb, Illinois, and Hilo, Hawaii, where they trained us.

Perhaps this is one reason I appreciate living in Paris. The benefits that Simmons taught us to analyse in his system included tolerance for non-conformists. Most of the people I admire and have talked about have more than a bit of rebel in them. My great models, Miller, Colette and so on, were survivors who carved out a world that reflected their intelligence, their passion for writing and love, their courage to cast aside convention. Their lives may have been chaotic at times, but they were seldom monotonous.

A photograph of Colette on a postcard sitting on my mantel shows her as an old woman with short curly, gray hair lying in bed with large luxurious pillows behind her and a writing table with books, tablet and pen across her lap. She looks very content, even though we know that she suffered from painful arthritis. This is how I would like to picture myself many years from now.

People do leave Paris. Those who do so usually go with sadness, tempered by the rich experience they take with them. Among my friends and acquaintances the reasons are often to do with the declining dollar, which makes the place very expensive compared with living in America. Some have better health coverage at home or, as old age creeps up on them, feel a need to be close to their families. Sometimes the illness or death of a loved one here or there forces the decision. But even then they mostly try to return to Paris for extended vacations.

Paris is a place to recreate your self. People truly forget, until someone or something jogs their memory, that they had another life somewhere, and not necessarily a bad one – just a life that is over for now, or is being blended into a new one.

The poet emerges. The photographer clicks away. Your hair is colored and cut. Your palate discerns new tastes. You stroll, instead of jumping into a car. You discover that Paris has jogging trails, tennis courts, magnificent parks, college alumni clubs, opera, theater, a diverse selection of films and eventually your favorite Café de la Mairie, with the pigeon lady down there out the window. You fall in love – perhaps not with someone, but with a life you've created.

Germaine de Staël, the great woman writer of Napoleon's era, who lived part of her life in Paris, once asked, 'What else is happiness but the development of our abilities?' The new abilities one develops here may be more abstract, about *being* rather than doing. Our senses may become sharper. We may dine leisurely for three hours, instead of eating and running. As aspirant writers or artists, we may acclaim our professions proudly, instead of making excuses about not having a real job. We may learn to pay attention to the details that enrich our lives rather than the material things that display our wealth.

In my neighborhood flower shop this morning I saw a French mother holding out a blue vase while her ten-year old son, holding a yellow linen napkin, helped the florist select flowers. 'Remember, Jean-Luc,' said the mother, 'grand-mère prefers simple but elegant arrangements.' Teaching him how to decorate the Sunday dinner table was an act of love and respect. We can learn from generations of this ingrained attention to aesthetic detail.

Henry Miller is no longer just under my bed. He is here in Paris, where the photographs from *My Life and Times* are being digitized, his manuscripts preserved and his audio tapes put on disc. And his writing and lifestyle of course still influence today's authors and dreamers who wander the streets, sometimes lost, sometimes not. His legacy lives on in many books which are now spared the censor's wrath or law's restraint. When the Supreme Court declared *Tropic of Cancer* to be a work of literature, Paris was adorned with yet another reflecting light whose glow and shadow can still be seen in its corners.

Hanging in the entry of my apartment are two signed lithographs from Henry's series of paintings in *Insomnia*. These gifts from Bradley Smith continually remind me of the value of friendship and importance of preserving a particular past.

Max Lerner taught me an important lesson. 'There are two things we have to do, Mary,' he said. 'One is to make a living and the other is to make a life. It is important to make a living. But it is more important to make a life.'

I am making mine now in Paris.

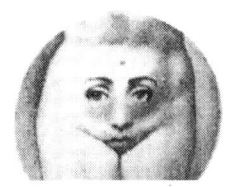